C000221837

CAN YOU PASS THE SEX TEST?

ANNE HOOPER

CAN YOU PASS THE SEX TEST?

ANNE HOOPER

London, New York, Munich, Melbourne, Delhi
A Penguin Company

Designed and edited by
Cooling Brown

Category Publisher Corinne Roberts
Senior Managing Art Editor Lynne Brown
Senior Editor Peter Jones
US Editor Margaret Parrish
DTP Karen Constanti
Production Sarah Sherlock
Jacket Editor Beth Apple
Jacket Designer Nathalie Godwin

First printed in Great Britain in 2002 by
Dorling Kindersley Ltd,
80 Strand, London WC2R ORL
2 4 6 8 10 9 7 5 3 1

Copyright © 2002
Dorling Kindersley Limited

All rights reserved, no part of this publication may be reproduced, stored in a retrieval system, or transmitted in any form or by any means, electronic, mechanical, photocopying, recording, or otherwise, without the prior permission of the copyright owner.

A CIP catalogue record for this book is available from the British Library.

ISBN 0 7513 1280 0

Reproduced by GRB, Italy
Printed and bound by Graphicon, Italy

See our complete catalogue at
www.dk.com

Contents

Introduction

I always enjoy doing psychological quizzes because they're a fun and easy way of finding out a little more about myself. And what could be more intriguing than finding out about your sexual self?

There are so many facets of your sexuality to think about. Do you think you are sexually knowledgeable, for example? Or are you an empathic lover, always thinking about your lover's experience and doing your best to enhance lovemaking in a way that is just right for him or her? How are you on sex techniques? Do you feel confident about getting to know a new lover? Or are you a slow

starter – someone who takes time to experience trust and to build up a head of sexual steam?

We all have very different sexual natures. In building a sexual relationship, part of the enjoyment lies in finding out about your partner's thoughts and desires. But it's fun to find out more about yourself at the same time.

This little book sets out, in a light-hearted fashion, to help you get to know yourself better. Once you've discovered more about your sexual personality, I'll refer you to appropriate mini-essays on aspects of sexual knowledge that you might like to explore.

At the very least I hope you find this a fun present to give your partner. At most, you just might discover your inner sexual desires burning away inside you, in time-honored volcanic fashion. Please read and enjoy.

All the very best,

Anne J. Hooper

ANNE HOOPER

part one **the**

sex test

Are you a **confident lover?**

Confidence is a very sexy quality, especially when flirtation and good humor are part of the package. In fact, confidence is key to sexiness because to feel good about sex, you need to feel good about yourself. Confidence is also catching – if one partner has it, he or she can instill it in the other. So how great do you feel about yourself and how does your self-assurance affect your lovemaking?

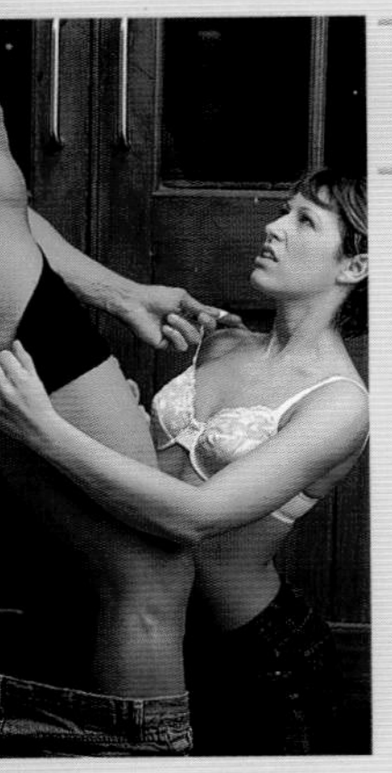

1 *You haven't yet had sex with your* **new** *partner, but you are dying to. On your* **next date**, *do you:*

a Pin your partner to the wall and say you have to have him/her now? ☐

b Tell your partner you'd like to take things further the next time you're alone together? ☐

c Wait until things start heating up and hope he/she takes the initiative? ☐

2 *Your partner is trying to* **stimulate** *you, but his/her technique isn't giving you much* **pleasure**. *Do you:*

a Whisper into your lover's ear and explain what you'd like him/her to do? ☐

b Guide your lover's hand with your own until he/she gets into the swing of it? ☐

c Let your lover carry on with what he/she is doing and hope it gets better? ☐

3 *You wake up next to your* **sleeping** *partner feeling very* **horny**. *Do you:*

a Gently sit on top of your lover, kiss his/her face, and whisper how much you want him/her? ☐

b Snuggle up close and tentatively stroke your lover until he/she becomes aroused? ☐

c Kiss your lover on the cheek and wait, trembling, for him/her to wake up? ☐

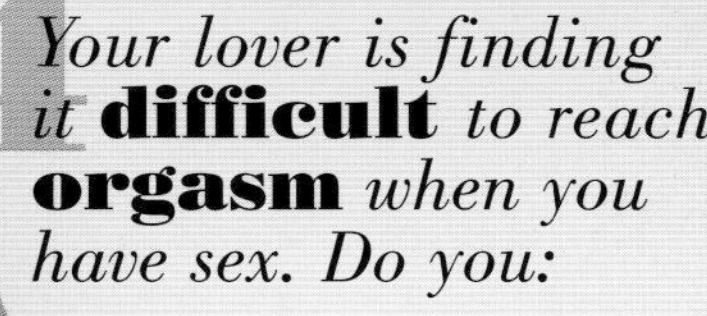

4 *Your lover is finding it* **difficult** *to reach* **orgasm** *when you have sex. Do you:*

a Talk about it matter-of-factly and work out techniques that may help? ☐

b Put more energy into your lovemaking and hope that will help? ☐

c Ride it out and hope things improve? ☐

5 *When you are giving your partner* **oral sex**, *do you:*

a Feel free to ask for guidance and for feedback? ☐

b Sometimes get it right, but rarely use it to bring your partner to orgasm? ☐

c Usually try to avoid that area unless your partner requests it – you're not confident you know what he/she likes? ☐

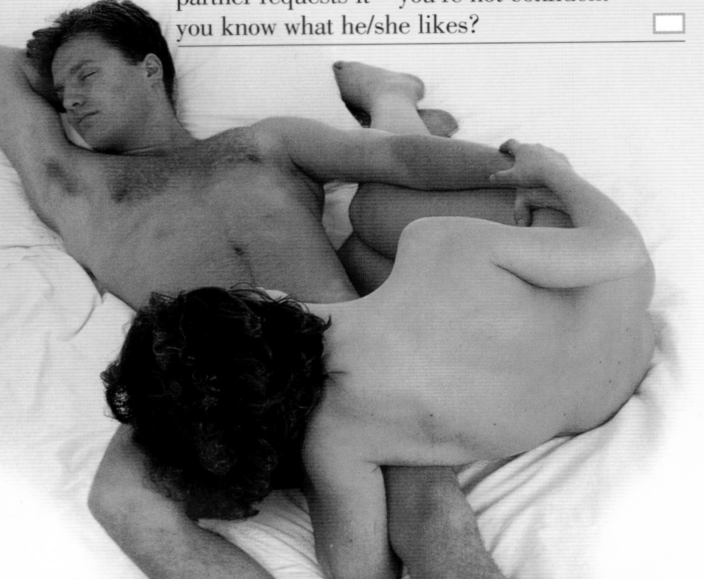

6 *When it comes to making the* **first move** *for sex, do you:*

- **a** Feel happy to take the initiative yourself? ☐
- **b** Sometimes get the ball rolling, but prefer it when your partner comes on strong? ☐
- **c** Always let your partner make the first move? ☐

7 *You're* **naked** *in bed with your new partner and you need to use the bathroom, but your bathrobe is* **nowhere** *to be seen. Do you:*

- **a** Climb out of bed in all your natural glory and saunter seductively across the room? ☐
- **b** Get out of bed and walk to the door as quickly as you can? ☐
- **c** Gather yourself up in the blanket and roll toward the door? ☐

8 *Your* **new partner** *doesn't seem to want sex as regularly as you do, and you're* **worried**. *Do you:*

a Talk to your partner about it and tell him/her that you hope there's nothing wrong? ☐

b Try to coax him/her into it a bit more often? ☐

c Wait it out and hope that things get better? ☐

9 *You're having intercourse and your* **partner** *wants to stop before you've* **climaxed**. *Do you:*

a Ask him/her to stimulate you manually until you are able to come? ☐

b Finish yourself off? ☐

c Stop and maybe try again a bit later? ☐

10 *When it comes to* **foreplay**, *do you usually begin by:*

a Kissing and gently touching the most sensitive and tantalizing areas of your partner's body? ☐

b Fondling and stroking his/her genital area and nipples? ☐

c Rhythmically rubbing your body up against your partner's? ☐

How **confident** are you?

Mostly As – supremely self-assured

You have a great self-image and are happy with the way you look and feel, which gives you the confidence to take the initiative in bed. You know what you want when it comes to sex and are not shy about getting it. You also have faith in your ability to satisfy your partner's sexual needs. Your lack of inhibition makes you a good listener – your partner can discuss sexual matters with you without embarrassment. You are bold enough to broach sensitive subjects and can ask your partner outright about his/her needs.

As far as sex is concerned, it is great to feel entirely comfortable. However, be aware that a more sexually inhibited partner may feel intimidated by you. Be careful not to be too overpowering – understand that some situations require taking a step back rather than a step forward. Take a look at **Reading sexual body language** (page 220).

Mostly Bs – fairly self-assured

Although your sexual confidence is quite high, you could enhance your love life by letting down a few defenses and taking the initiative a little more. You enjoy sex and are fairly certain about what makes your partner tick. You take the initiative when you need to and usually hit the right spot. However, sometimes you're unsure about how to proceed because you don't want to ask. At times you also feel reluctant to speak up about your own desires and express what you want. You may find it helpful to look at **Reading sexual body language** (page 220).

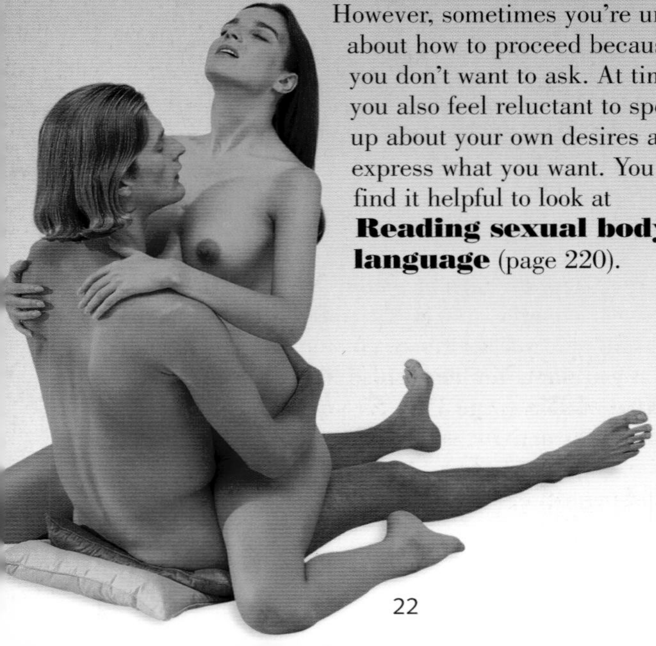

Improving your personal sexual knowledge may also help you take the initiative, since you will feel confident that you are making the right moves. Learn about your partner's erogenous zones by playing the **Map test game** (page 164).

Mostly Cs – a little unsure

Although you may be happy with your sex life as it stands, it could seriously improve if you addressed some of your confidence issues. You may have a healthy desire for sex, but you don't feel entirely happy about asking for it. Don't be afraid to make a move on your partner – all men and women love to be approached. (Women who think men don't like them to make sexual advances might be interested to know that the opposite is true!)

I suggest you try an exercise called **Stepping** (page 228), which allows you to tackle difficult tasks in stages and should help you feel more comfortable about asking for what you want. You might also like a few tips on **Kissing skills** (page 174). Kissing is probably the least scary sex activity, and, if you do it right, everything's possible. I know one woman who climaxes from kissing alone.

Are you an **intimate lover?**

Sexual intimacy is a wonderful feeling – but one that can be eroded in an instant by a single thoughtless comment or show of impatience. If you give out little caring or warmth, your sexual relationship will miss out on its most meaningful ingredient and is unlikely to realize its full potential. So how good are you at lowering the barriers and establishing sexual intimacy?

1 *Before you and your partner have sex, do you* **caress** *each other's bodies?*

a Always – it's an important part of building up to sex. ☐

b Sometimes, when the mood strikes you. ☐

c As much as is required to warm things up for intercourse. ☐

2 *Do you consider* **oral** *sex:*

a An important and regular part of your lovemaking? ☐

b An occasional part of your sex life? ☐

c Something that you rarely indulge in? ☐

3 *After you* **make love**, *do you:*

a Snuggle up and hold your partner all night? ☐

b Enjoy a kiss and some hugs and then settle down to sleep on your side of the bed? ☐

c Roll over and go to sleep? ☐

4 *You* **want** *to try out a* **new** *sexual position. Do you:*

a Hungrily suggest it to your partner the next time you see him/her? ☐

b Wait until you're in bed and suggest you try it out? ☐

c Try to maneuver your partner into it when the moment of intercourse arrives? ☐

5 *You come home to find your partner soaking in a* **bubble bath**. *Do you:*

a Strip off and jump in? ☐

b Ask if he/she would like a back scrub? ☐

c Moan that all the hot water has been used up? ☐

6 *Your partner* **asks** *a question about your sexual* **history**. *Do you:*

a Happily spill the beans in detail? ☐

b Let slip a few tantalizing clues? ☐

c Feel paranoid and refuse to give a straight answer? ☐

7 *You step out of the* **shower** *and, as you grab a* **towel**, *your partner walks into the bathroom. Do you:*

a Pull your partner toward you and ask him/her to dry you off? ☐

b Dry yourself off and talk to him/her while he uses the bathroom? ☐

c Ask for some privacy and lock the door this time? ☐

8 *Your* **ideal** *night in with your* **partner** *would be:*

a Watching a sexy video in bed and making love during the hot spots? ☐

b Snuggling up on the sofa, then somehow finding yourself making love on the living room floor? ☐

c Enjoying a beer, takeout, the TV, quick sex, and passing out immediately in bed? ☐

9 *You think you might be* **falling in love** *with your new partner. Do you:*

a Tell him/her the next time you meet? ☐

b Wait until your partner tells you that he/she loves you and then say it back? ☐

c Don't feel you need to say it at all on the grounds that he/she must be able to tell? ☐

10 *When you and your partner are* **out** *on the town* **together**, *do you:*

a Like to hold hands, hug, and kiss, regardless of the company? ☐

b Hold hands occasionally but never in front of people you know? ☐

c Keep that sort of thing strictly for home? ☐

How **intimate** are you?

Mostly As – close as can be

You are entirely at ease with yourself, which allows you to get really close to your lover. You are willing to take risks with your feelings in order to cement the bond of sensuality. You value intimacy and are open and accepting, both physically and emotionally. Be aware, however, that in opening up so much, you risk getting hurt. Are you sure your partner is truly trustworthy enough to merit the priceless emotional gift you are bestowing?

You're already skilled in the art of intimacy, but you might be interested in expanding your sexual repertoire. See **Fun sex positions** (page 148), **Genital massage** (page 182), and **Oral sex** (page 196).

Mostly Bs – close and yet so far

Although you are open in many ways, you'd like to improve intimacy with your partner but lack confidence to take things further. Often, you'll wait for your partner to offer a gesture of closeness before you feel ready to open up – this may be a defense mechanism because you fear rejection. It's worth considering the "give to get" principle: If you offer warmth and intimacy, you are more likely to receive it because that is usually how others respond. If you need help to get more intimate with your lover, you may find the sections on **Oral sex** (page 196) and **Massage skills** (page 176) exactly what you need. Or, if you figure

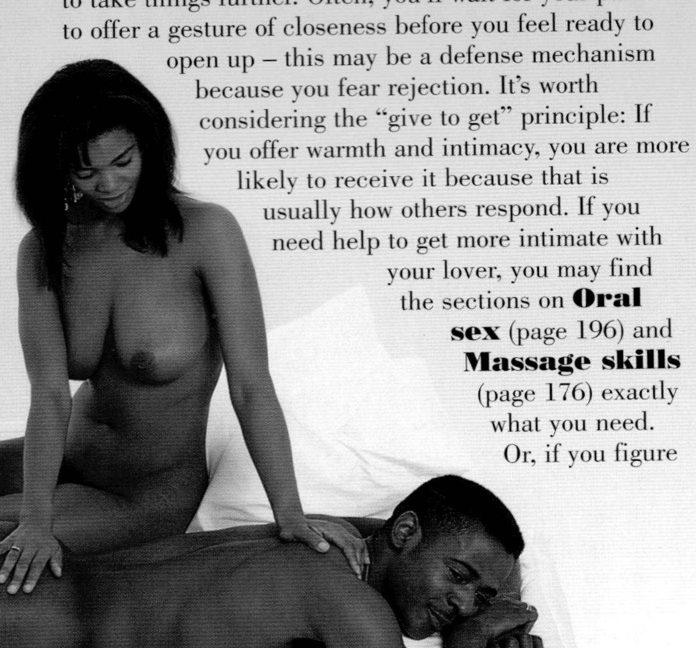

you know all these maneuvers already, take a look at **Genital massage** (page 182). Sexual intimacy is also about how you relax together. The **Sex history exercise** (page 224) will help you open up to each other and find out what makes you both tick sexually.

Mostly Cs – could be closer

You'd probably argue that sexual intimacy is unimportant to you – but that would be because, so far, you have experienced little of it. Usually, people who have yet to discover the joy of real relaxation with their lover (and therefore real trust – a vital ingredient of intimacy) are frightened. Perhaps at some time in your life you have learned to fear and distrust the opposite sex. Occasionally, this fear shows itself in being overly sexual.

You would gain a great deal by becoming comfortable with the more intimate aspects of the sex act. An invaluable exercise is the **Sexological exam** (page 222) in which you look at your partner's body in microscopic detail, get close to areas you may think of as dirty or messy, and talk through your feelings. You may each feel you are taking some risk in doing the exercise. That's fine. Risk-taking prevents us from dying of boredom. Better still, it encourages us to feel stimulated by each other.

Are you an **erotic lover?**

Being erotic is not necessarily about always being spontaneous or ready for instant sex. Eroticism can be premeditated – it lives in the mind as well as in the body and is often fueled by the power of suggestion. There is eroticism in game-playing, yet there is also eroticism in that connecting glance across a crowded room. But eroticism is mainly about turning on your lover's mind so much that his or her body loses control. It is even about delaying sexual satisfaction. It's quite an art.

1 *You're out to* **dinner** *with your partner and you suddenly get a twinge of* **desire**. *Do you:*

a Rub your fingers up and down your lover's thigh and say you can't wait to get him/her home? ☐

b Take your lover's hands in yours and stroke them while gazing into his/her eyes? ☐

c Take a forkful of food and think about what you'll do to him/her – only later? ☐

2 *Your partner has been* **away** *for a few days but is coming to your place* **tonight**. *Do you:*

a Open the door wearing your sexiest underwear? ☐

b Plan to get him/her into bed at the first opportunity? ☐

c Leave the door slightly open and arrange your naked self seductively on the bed? ☐

3 *You're* **walking** *in the woods with your partner and a* **lustful** *mood takes you. Do you:*

a Seduce your partner onto a soft patch of grass and proceed with getting sexy, even though you know there is the risk of being spotted? ☐

b Get very hot and steamy but stop short of giving a sex exhibition? ☐

c Suggest you head home to take things further? ☐

4 *Your partner's* **away** *on business and calls you late at night from a* **hotel** *room. Do you:*

a Ask your partner if he/she would like to hear an erotic story, and then tell it? ☐

b Whisper huskily into the receiver, describing what you're wearing and what you'd do if he/she were physically present? ☐

c Whisper into the receiver that you are making love to yourself? ☐

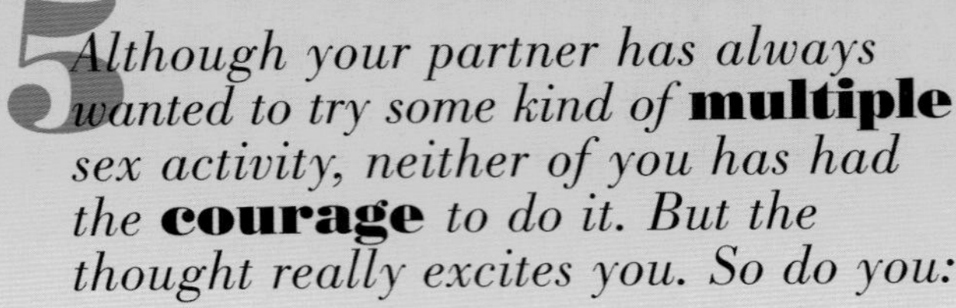

5 *Although your partner has always wanted to try some kind of* **multiple** *sex activity, neither of you has had the* **courage** *to do it. But the thought really excites you. So do you:*

a Explore an Internet chat room specially designated for sex and see what comments you arouse when you put on a virtual sex display? ☐

b Invent a sex scenario in which you are being ravished/doing the ravishing in front of a group of strangers? ☐

c Invest in full-length mirrors for the bedroom? ☐

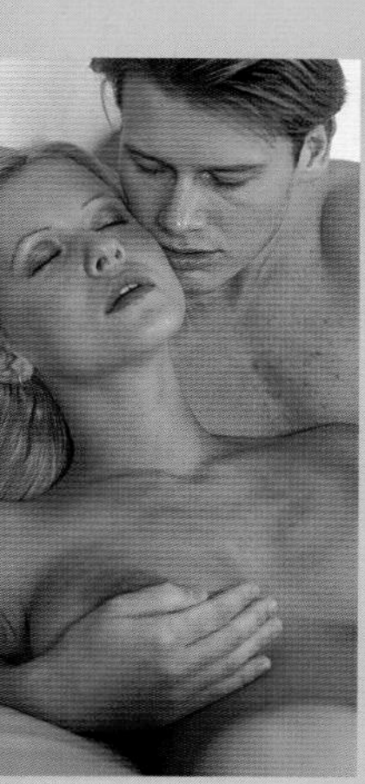

6 *You and your partner are* **lying** *in* **bed** *and you want to have sex. Do you:*

a Tell your partner very deliberately exactly what it is you would like to do to him/her, and then do it? ☐

b Gently and slowly caress his/her body and cover it with moist, breathy kisses? ☐

c Go single-mindedly at the genitals? ☐

7 *Your partner* **gives** *you a single* **red** *rose for Valentine's Day. Do you:*

a Stroke the flower over your partner's naked body that night, even though the thorns may pose a danger? ☐

b Strew the petals across the bed and start to peel off your clothes seductively? ☐

c Offer a grateful kiss and put the flower in a vase? ☐

8 *You and your partner are dying to have sex, but you're at a* **dinner** *party at a friend's* **house**. *Do you:*

a Signal to your partner to meet you in the bathroom, then kiss his/her neck and ears, whisper how much you want him/her, and send your lover back to the dinner table in a state of arousal? ☐

b Get your partner to meet you in the bathroom for a quickie? ☐

c Sit it out and pounce on him/her as soon as you get home? ☐

9 *After a* **romantic** *meal* à deux, *your partner offers you ice cream as a* **delicious** *dessert. Do you:*

a Smear some on your partner's stomach and slowly lick it off? ☐

b Get a spoon and feed your partner? ☐

c Get two spoons and eat it together? ☐

10

You and your partner are watching a **hot** *movie at home, and you are getting very* **turned on**. *Do you:*

a Get steamy on the sofa as the movie flickers in the background, to the point where the movie plot becomes extraneous? ☐

b Switch off the movie and lead your partner to the bedroom? ☐

c Wait until the movie's over and then get busy? ☐

How **erotic** are you?

Mostly As – subtle yet steamy

You possess an interesting combination of subtlety and passion. You realize that holding back can provoke far more erotic desire than instantly rushing in, yet you don't hesitate to show your warmth of feeling. You're a sensualist who believes in spending hours on good sex, but you understand that every sex act needs a good beginning – a beginning where you give a partner time to turn on. You understand that not everyone feels exactly as you do, which means you have the potential to be a really great lover.

While you will not need advice on sensual moves, you might be interested in playing some erotic games. Game-playing may seem premeditated, but the experience does not have to be artificial. The emotions we bring to games are what count. Take a look at **The big stick** (page 140), **Bad slave game** (page 138), and **Sexual initiation rites** (page 136).

Mostly Bs – tantalizingly hot

You are passionate and driven, with an inventive mind and a good appetite for ice cream, loving, and rosebuds! For you, a more direct approach works well, and you are not afraid to explore novelty. But you most certainly do not want to risk going public in any way – sex is a private pursuit for you. That said, you are not averse to a quickie when there's a risk of interruption, provided there is a lock on the door! You are not afraid to express love in public, although there's a limit as to how far this is allowed to go. You are generally open to suggestions, especially from someone you find wonderful.

You won't want to go as far as experimenting with bondage or anything that might cause pain. But you might have fun with a **Sexy photo session** (page 156), where the pictures do not need to be viewed by anyone other than yourself and your lover. Or, writing **Sexy love notes** (page 154) might be just what's needed to put ideas into your partner's head. Or take a look at **Shower power** (page 158).

Mostly Cs – spontaneously warm

You are full of good ideas and enthusiasm. And there is nothing like enthusiasm for being a spontaneous turn-on in itself. You are dying to explore new sexual avenues and are happy to make real changes to add that extra something to your bedroom behavior. You are a happy voyeur and exhibitionist, but you are careful not to expose yourself to anyone else but your lover's eyes.

Enhancing eroticism for you would expand your enjoyment of your natural and spontaneous sexuality. Feast on a **Sexual banquet** (page 150) and see **Birthday treats** (page 144), where I suggest you do something out of character (such as dressing up as the opposite sex and going out on a public date). You might experience something really different and arousing. Go for it!

Are you a **skillful lover?**

Many people think that good sex just happens – that we intuitively know what to do. Unfortunately, they are wrong. Of course, it's great when you can gauge instinctively what thrills a partner, but this is a rare occurrence and certainly not the norm. We all need to learn basic lovemaking skills somewhere along the way. Ideally, we do so with a partner we love. So, what kind of skills do you possess as a lover?

1 *When it comes to* **oral** *sex, do you:*

a Always bring your partner to orgasm or close to orgasm with deliberate strokes of your silky mouth? ☐

b Enjoy it as part of your lovemaking but don't guarantee it will work? ☐

c Occasionally indulge in it, but not for very long? ☐

2 *Your new partner is* **inhibited** *but wants to get* **close**. *Do you:*

a Accept that it may take weeks before it feels right to go to bed and focus on a slow courtship instead? ☐

b Buy a couple of sex books and leave them lying around in the hope that he/she will pick them up, read them, and grow more comfortable with the subject? ☐

c Take him/her to bed early on in the relationship on the grounds that it's best to get things over with? ☐

3

You are about to **orgasm** *during intercourse but your partner is still a long way from climax and you want to* **delay** *things so you can manage it together. Do you:*

a Slow things down and concentrate for a few seconds before feeling safe enough to continue? ☐

b Try to slow things down, but know this may not work? ☐

c Give in – you can stimulate your partner to his/her own climax manually, if need be? ☐

4 *Your lover is about to* **orgasm** *during intercourse and you want to make it* **wonderful**. *Do you:*

a Continue with what you're doing; it's obviously working? ☐

b Use your body to give him/her as much friction and intensity as you can, while breathing something sexy into his/her ear? ☐

c Bring yourself to the point of orgasm, so that you can enjoy the ecstatic release together? ☐

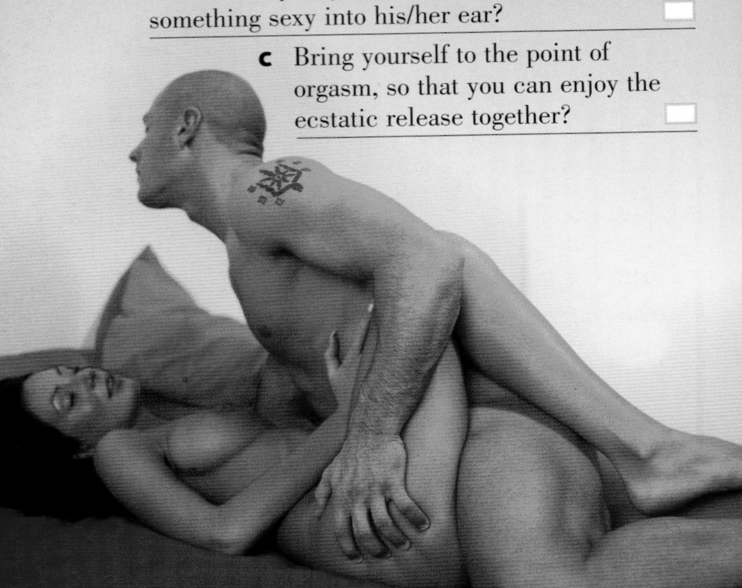

5 *When enjoying* **foreplay**, *do you:*

a Drive your partner wild by kissing and touching in all the places you know are right for him/her? ☐

b Kiss and touch your partner and listen out for his/her responses? ☐

c Concentrate on the genital areas and the nipples, which are bound to be sensitive? ☐

6 *You're trying a new sex* **position**, *but your partner is finding it a little* **uncomfortable**. *Do you:*

a Gently guide his/her body around and alter your own position until he/she settles into it? ☐

b Ask him/her what you can do to make it more comfortable? ☐

c Give up – this one obviously isn't for you? ☐

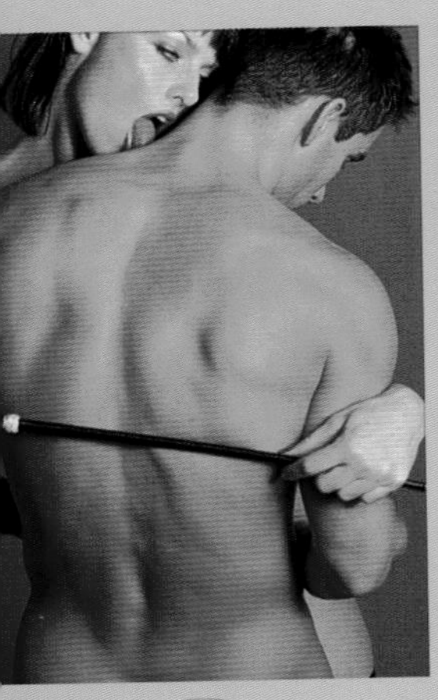

7 *Your* **partner** *really adores a sex* **activity** *that you dislike. Do you:*

a Distract your partner by giving such amazing alternative sex that he/she forgets about the original request?

b Do the sex activity begrudgingly, gritting your teeth as you proceed?

c Refuse point blank, leaving no room for negotiation?

8 *Your partner finds it* **difficult** *to* **climax**. *Do you:*

a Ask him/her what you can do to make climax easier, and have fun in experimenting?

b Increase the speed and amount of stimulation you are giving your lover on the grounds that he/she may not be getting enough?

c Refuse to worry: You feel that time will improve things?

9 *How would your partner describe* **you** *in* **bed?**

a Fantastic – the best lover he/she's ever had? ☐

b Pretty damn good? ☐

c You'd have to ask him/her? ☐

10 *On the subject of your lover's* **G-spot** *or* **prostate** *gland, do you:*

a Know exactly where it is and how to use it to drive your partner crazy with ecstasy? ☐

b Have a fair idea of its location, but it's all a bit hit or miss? ☐

c Mean to research it one day but keep putting it off? ☐

How **skillful** are you?

Mostly As – technical whiz

Your technical skills in bed are awesome. You are sensitive, knowledgeable, practiced, and unafraid of new ideas. You don't mind taking any amount of time to find out what works and what doesn't for your lover. You feel comfortable and relaxed enough to tackle sexual difficulties without fuss. In fact, you are probably an ideal partner.

My only warning is that your lovemaking might come across as staged. There is a thin line between skillful sex and artificiality, and you risk losing spontaneity if you over-rely on technique.

Believe it or not, the perfect lover is one who gets it wrong occasionally! You might enjoy learning about ancient **Tantric sex** (page 208).

Mostly Bs – well qualified

You are always learning and keep an open mind when it comes to discovering new skills. People who leave sex books around are often those who most want to read them. Nothing wrong with that. Sex books titillate but also inform. But you are a little unconfident. Perhaps you need to hone up on some of your basic lovemaking skills, not because what you've done so far is poor – not at all. But because by getting so much of your lovemaking right, you stand a great chance of transforming it further.

I suggest you take a look at **Oral sex** (page 196) as well as **Masturbation during intercourse** (page 204). You probably know all these details, but sometimes going over old ground helps reaffirm your knowledge so that you feel more confident.

Mostly Cs – learning all the time

You are an engaging mix of sympathy, optimism, and enthusiasm. You have all the right instincts, although your lovemaking skills occasionally fall short. It could be that you are lazy or even anxious about learning new skills. If something sexual feels threatening, for example, we often mysteriously put off trying it. When we don't try, we can't fail. But be reassured – really good lovers do make mistakes – and enjoy learning from them.

You also tend to give up easily when things don't go entirely well. Faced with something you dislike, you dig in your heels so hard that there is never any room for negotiation. This is a pity because it means you miss out. If you could relax some of your fixed ideas about sex and agree to experiment tentatively, if only once, you might discover some great new experiences.

I think you would gain from the **Sexological exam** (page 222) – especially if there are aspects of your partner's body that make you feel a bit squeamish. The **Map test game** (page 164) will help you discover the parts of your lover's body that do and don't respond to touch. For a treat, try the **Soapsud massage** (page 188). Above all, have fun fooling around.

Are you a **learned lover?**

Understanding sexual response is vital. We need a good knowledge of how the body works so that we can help it to work better. And getting to grips with the biology of sex doesn't hurt either. But lovemaking is not all about biology. If you use your practical sexual knowledge to please your lover, you are likely to end up pretty damn hot in bed. So do you qualify as a learned lover?

1 *You know that men usually find it* **easier** *and* **quicker** *to reach orgasm than women, barring some obvious exceptions. Do you therefore:*

a Keep a vibrator by the side of the bed in case she needs assistance in catching up? ☐

b Spend far longer on foreplay for her than for him? ☐

c Expect to speak up about special needs on the grounds that the man can't be expected to know everything? ☐

2 *You're* **contemplating** *sex with a new partner but are* **concerned** *about possible HIV infection. Do you:*

a Figure that the safest thing to do is to use condoms and avoid the discussion? ☐

b Admit you have had an HIV test and ask your new partner to do the same? ☐

c Figure there is so little likelihood of infection that it's probably worth taking a chance? ☐

3 *Your partner has* **contracted** *a sexually transmitted disease (STD). Do you:*

a Realize that this could be an unfortunate leftover from a former relationship? ☐

b Look at your own sexual hygiene? ☐

c Decide that your partner has been cheating on you? ☐

4 *If your partner's level of* **arousal** *dwindles during foreplay, do you:*

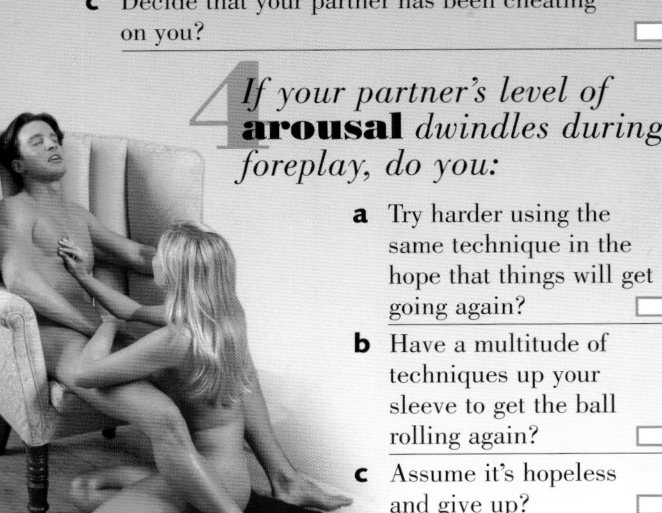

a Try harder using the same technique in the hope that things will get going again? ☐

b Have a multitude of techniques up your sleeve to get the ball rolling again? ☐

c Assume it's hopeless and give up? ☐

5 *Knowing that* **men** *take longer to* **re-arouse** *after orgasm, do you:*

a Believe the woman should hurry up and do this by stimulating herself? ☐

b Delay the man's arousal and concentrate solely on hers to begin with? ☐

c Let the man climax anyway on the grounds that he will surely manage another erection quickly if he is that fast? ☐

6 *You are finding it* **difficult** *to* **orgasm** *during sex. Do you:*

a Try a clever new position designed to increase sensation? ☐

b Take much longer enjoying foreplay? ☐

c Increase oral and manual stimulation because your partner is missing out on local stimulation? ☐

7 *When it comes to your lover's* **erogenous** *zones, have you:*

a Always known that the genitals and the nipples are key areas? ☐

b Discovered exactly which areas feel sensational for him/her specifically? ☐

c Felt worried because you don't know where the erogenous zones are? ☐

8 *If you/your man* **suffers** *from an episode of* **impotence**, *do you:*

a Shrug it off on the grounds that it happens to everyone at some time in his life? ☐

b Blame it on certain circumstances or even a certain partner? ☐

c Worry that your/his sexual powers are waning due to age or illness? ☐

9 *Knowing that the* **clitoris** *is the key to a woman's sexual sensation, would you* **stimulate** *it by:*

a Rubbing it directly on the head ☐

b Rubbing it to one side or the other? ☐

c Rubbing it in circles? ☐

10 *To* **delay** *your man's* **orgasm** *would you:*

a Slow down sex when it seems necessary? ☐

b Give his penis the "squeeze technique"? ☐

c Experiment with an anesthetic spray? ☐

How **learned** are you?

Mostly As – hazy on the facts

You want to know more about sex and the human body and are already using your common sense to come up with some well-meaning solutions. You are relaxed about the occasional sexual difficulty, so if things don't work out quite right you're not one to panic. You are open-minded and flexible enough to apply your knowledge in the way you think best.

But you haven't got all your facts quite right. You know, for example, that the clitoris is the female hot spot, but you may not yet have discovered that (usually) the best way to stimulate it is from the side. You understand that there is a need to prevent orgasm when the man suffers from premature ejaculation, but may not know the best way to go about this. Take a look at **Clitoral stimulation** (page 190), **Condom know-how** (page 172), and **Slowing him down** (page 206). Put these subjects into practice and you back your willingness up with real, tried-and-true information.

Mostly Bs – the fount of knowledge

You know your sex facts well and use them intelligently. There's not much you don't know about the human body, and the men/women in your life have a lot to be thankful for. You understand, for example, that the best way to slow down the male orgasm without sacrificing sensation is to firmly block climax by squeezing the penis.

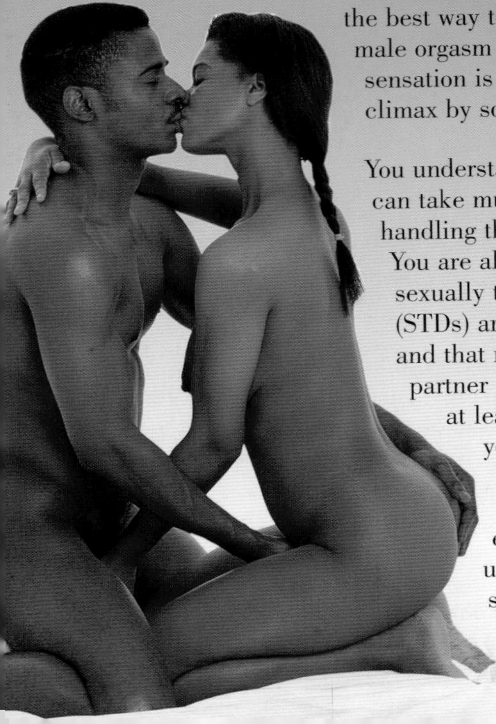

You understand that the penis can take much tougher handling than many realize. You are also well aware that sexually transmitted diseases (STDs) are easily contracted and that rather than your partner infecting you, it is at least as feasible that you may have infected him/her. You are mature enough to understand that slower sex is the key to better sex – at least where many women are concerned. You would probably learn more again from taking a look at **Safer sex** (page 170), **Impotence solutions** (page 216), and **Sex pills** (page 218). The advice here would be to hone the skills you already possess.

Mostly Cs – student days

You are at an early point in understanding how sex works. You feel worried because you think you should know more about sex technique and health – indeed certain situations make you uneasy at present. We all want to become better lovers, and knowing what sex is about also raises our confidence. The good news is that it is fun going to sex school.

One couple I counseled actually pretended to be students again and sat and studied in the evening. Their activity was not entirely serious, you'll be glad to hear. They tested each other's general sexual knowledge and deducted points for wrong answers. The loser had to pay a sexual forfeit of the winner's choosing. The only snag was that there was a built-in advantage to getting the answers wrong! Test your own knowledge by taking a look at **Did you know...** (page 168).

Are you a **thoughtful lover?**

A selfish lover doesn't give two hoots about a partner's welfare. A thoughtful one, in contrast, rapidly picks up a lover's desires and then shows that he or she has done so by acting on what has been learned. If you don't ever tell a partner "I love you," or never do anything designed to show your affection, how else will he or she ever know you care? So just how thoughtful a lover do you consider yourself to be?

1 *Your partner has been rather* **withdrawn** *lately. Do you:*

a Make the time to listen and encourage your partner to say what's on his/her mind? ☐

b Ask him/her what's the matter between phone calls? ☐

c Tell him/her to snap out of it – other people are in far worse situations? ☐

2 *Your partner has put on* **weight** *and is feeling self-conscious. Do you:*

a Cover your lover with kisses from head to toe to show how gorgeous you think he/she is? ☐

b Say you still find him/her as attractive as ever? ☐

c Find it much harder to get sexy? ☐

3 *Your partner wants to have sex but has been finding it* **difficult** *to get* **aroused** *lately. Do you:*

a Plan a relaxed evening at home and treat him/her to a sensual massage with absolutely no sexual performance required at all? ☐

b Stimulate his/her nipples and genital area to see if you can turn him/her on? ☐

c Get upset that he/she no longer finds you attractive? ☐

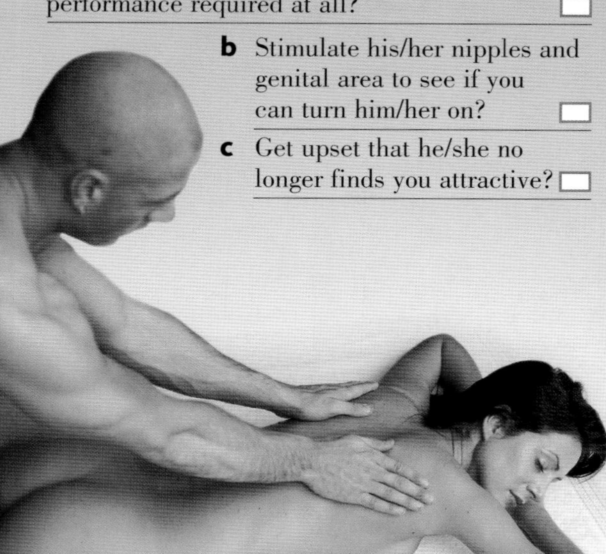

4 *Your partner is going* **away** *for a few days and this is your last* **night** *together. Do you:*

a Plan a romantic evening at home followed by a night of passion? ☐

b Go out for a few drinks, then come home and fall into bed together? ☐

c Go out on your own, but try not to get home too late so you get the opportunity to tell your partner you'll miss him/her? ☐

5 *Your partner dresses up in some "erotic" new* **underwear**, *but you think it looks* **terrible**. *Do you:*

a Tell your lover he/she looks absolutely gorgeous and rip off the underwear in a lustful frenzy? ☐

b Say he/she doesn't need underwear to look great? ☐

c Laugh and ask if he/she still has the receipt? ☐

6 *Your partner has been finding sex* **painful** *lately. Do you:*

a Accompany him/her to the doctor and tackle the problem together? ☐

b Suggest that he/she go to the doctor to find out what's wrong? ☐

c Hope that the problem will go away? ☐

7 *You don't really* **enjoy** *your partner's* **favorite** *sexual position. Do you:*

a Indulge him/her often ?

b Do it sometimes?

c Try to avoid the position?

8 *You love having sex with the* **lights on**, *but your partner doesn't. Do you:*

a Resort to romantic candles placed discreetly around the bedroom?

b Agree to just having a lamp on occasionally?

c Resign yourself to sex in the dark?

9 *Your partner wants to* **stop** *just as you're nearing* **climax**. *Do you:*

a Stop and ask him/her what's wrong?

b Keep going but ask him/her what's wrong the minute you've climaxed?

c Get angry and say bitter words you come to regret afterward?

10 *It's* **Valentine's Day** *and you want to show your lover how much you* **care**. *Do you:*

a Take your partner out for an expensive dinner and shower him/her with romantic gifts? ☐

b Buy him/her the biggest and best card you can find, but do no more? ☐

c Send an electronic Valentine's card that is in dubious taste? ☐

How **thoughtful** are you?

Mostly As – so considerate!

You are the soul of sensitivity and discretion, yet you refuse to be a doormat. When disagreements occur, you can come up with a subtle compromise and avoid a major battle. When your partner digs his or her heels in over a sexual issue, you know just how to bring him/her round. You are good at initiating sex, understanding the value of romance in a relationship. In short, you are the most thoughtful of lovers. Just one word of caution. Don't pander to a partner's moods to the extent that he or she governs everything you do. There will be times when you need to be in the spotlight and when it is you who wants to play an interesting sex game – so make sure you do.

You might enjoy knowing more about the impact of different types of sexy dressing. There are many ways of setting the mood for lovemaking through the use of clothes, lighting, and props. Why not try something new? Take a look at **Dressing up for sex** (page 142) for some intriguing inspiration.

Mostly Bs – strong and caring

You are thoughtful and caring, but you are your own person. You try to fulfill your lover's wishes, but you won't be pushed around. This is because you possess a strong sense of what is fair and what is not. If necessary, you will act against your own desires in order to accommodate a lover, which is rare. You are warm, reassuring, and happy to show appreciation.

However, you don't always tune in as sensitively as you could. Perhaps this is because you expect your partner to think and feel much the same as you do. Since we all hail from very different families and therefore very different value systems, this is illogical. Try an exercise called **Romantic reminiscences** (page 226) to help you learn about each other's sexual history and see how past experience shapes your expectations for the future.

Mostly Cs – longing to care

You are longing for a relationship in which you feel genuinely in tune with your partner. Nothing would suit you better than to feel on exactly the same wavelength – both in and out of bed. But you have hit some hurdles along the way in the shape of depression, incomprehension, and sheer bad luck. So you are a little discouraged. Possibly some of the problem lies in what you expect from a relationship. Perhaps you believe that a partner should be thoughtful on your account yet have so little experience of this in your own life that you are not sure how to reciprocate. But you would like to learn!

There are some basic behavioral moves that will help you acquire sexual insight. Take a look at **Ten thoughts to remember** (page 232). Stick to these, and you will see an instant improvement in your partner's reaction to you. Odds are that he/she will become more loving and appreciative. That, in turn, will make you feel like a million dollars. And we all want to feel like that.

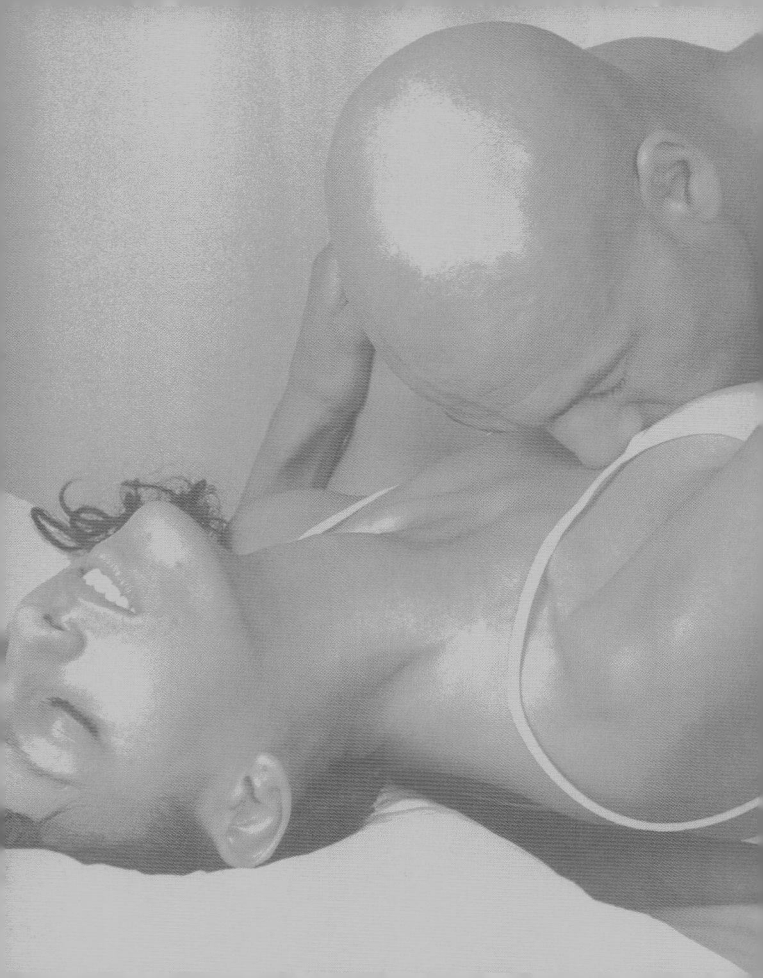

Are you a **powerful lover?**

When applied to sex, power is about presence rather than sexual stamina. People with sexual power are completely at one with themselves. While women are deeply attracted to powerful men, men tend to be wary of powerful women, seeing them as competition. Powerful women therefore learn to temper their strength by being warm and welcoming but unwilling to put up with any nonsense. Truly powerful men tend to be the same. So how do you rate yourself?

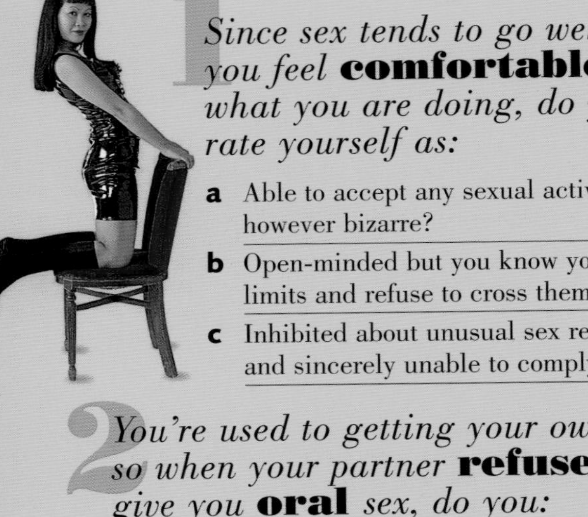

1 *Since sex tends to go well when you feel* **comfortable** *with what you are doing, do you rate yourself as:*

a Able to accept any sexual activity, however bizarre? ☐

b Open-minded but you know your own limits and refuse to cross them? ☐

c Inhibited about unusual sex requests and sincerely unable to comply? ☐

2 *You're used to getting your own way, so when your partner* **refuses** *to give you* **oral** *sex, do you:*

a Feel that you are being denied something vital to your well-being and go into a serious sulk? ☐

b Understand that this partner is inhibited or prejudiced and set about offering him/her oral sex instead on the grounds that he/she can be helped to get comfortable with the whole concept? ☐

c Accept the lack of interest but make a mental note to move on from the relationship soon? ☐

3 *Imagine you are* **interested** *in S&M* **games** *and want to introduce your new partner to these. Do you:*

a Feel that the best way to get a partner comfortable with the S&M scene is to take him/her to a party so he/she can get firsthand experience? ☐

b Seduce your partner into light bondage games with silken ropes and promises of sexual treats to come, in the comfort of your own home? ☐

c Talk about the delights of S&M in nonsexual surroundings, such as in a bar, as a kind of introduction? ☐

4 *Imagine that all you have to do to* **arouse** *your partner is simply to breathe on him/her. The* **response** *is absolutely guaranteed. Do you:*

a Find yourself turning him/her on anytime you feel like sex? ☐

b Wait for your partner to approach you? ☐

c Find your partner's instant response ultimately boring? ☐

5 *If you were to rate how important* **sex** *is to you compared with other factors in your* **life***, would it be:*

a more important? ☐

b about the same? ☐

c less important? ☐

6 *As we* **grow older***, sex often becomes less* **sensational***, partly through habituation, partly through maturity. Would you:*

a Have as much sex as possible on the grounds that it keeps you young? ☐

b Enjoy terrific sex but less often than before? ☐

c Change partners on the grounds that a newer, younger lover is more of an aphrodisiac? ☐

7 *When it comes to calling the* **shots** *during lovemaking, do you:*

a Love to take control and direct the action? ☐

b Often take control, but don't mind when your partner takes the lead? ☐

c Usually let your partner take control? ☐

8 *If you had little* **time** *for a sexual relationship, partners might find this difficult to* **cope** *with. Would you:*

a Set up a relationship but expect it to be limited because it never gets much time to expand? ☐

b Keep trying to find a great new partner on the grounds that, one day, someone will understand and cope with your time problem? ☐

c Accept that personal relationships won't get much of a role to play in your life? ☐

9 *If you* **suggested** *to your partner that you'd like to experiment, such as by taking part in a* **threesome**, *do you think he/she would:*

a Immediately cooperate? ☐

b Feel free to say "yes" or "no"? ☐

c Reluctantly cooperate? ☐

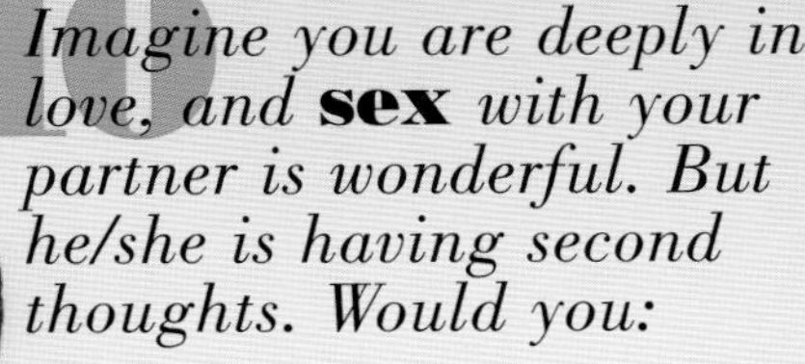

10 *Imagine you are deeply in love, and* **sex** *with your partner is wonderful. But he/she is having second thoughts. Would you:*

a Feel despair over the possibility of losing your partner and beg him/her not to leave? ☐

b Console yourself with the fact that you have loved deeply but you can't win them all? ☐

c Defend yourself by instantly finding a new lover? ☐

How **powerful** are you?

Mostly As – gaining power

You are a very attractive person but have some way to go as a powerful man or woman. Sex is extremely important to you, perhaps because you are not really quite certain of your attractiveness. When sex goes well, you don't necessarily trust in it or in yourself. You are bored by too much success and yet you sometimes behave like a child when, against the odds, a relationship doesn't work out.

Although you love the physical sensation of sex, you don't always see your partner as an individual. And while you appear to be happy to devote time to his/her sexual well-being, at heart you resent having to make such a time commitment. You are a strange mixture of personal success and yet somehow being trapped in that success. It might interest you to know that personal priorities alter as we get older. Ambition in the workplace, very important during youth and middle age, often becomes meaningless in midlife if love relationships are

unsatisfactory. The point of these observations is that however powerful the personality, life still needs to have balance. Love and sex need to ride along with ambition, not instead of it. You might be interested in **Impotence solutions** (page 216), and **Safer sex** (page 170).

Mostly Bs – mighty impressive

You are a truly powerful personality. You're relaxed in your attitude toward the opposite sex, you value relationships, and although you have the power to manipulate people, you deliberately refrain from doing so because you want to be loved freely and spontaneously. You know full well that should people respond against their nature, you may feel powerful but you won't feel truly loved.

Since you have limitations on your time, you will want to make the most of the opportunities that arise. You may find the **Weekend break** (page 162) and the **Soapsud massage** (page 188) helpful.

Mostly Cs – power needs mastering

You are powerful, but you still need maturity in order to handle such power well. Sex for you is more about the act than the relationship. But the trouble with this attitude is that sex, on its own, however incredible for your partner, gets boring; plus, you see sex partners as replaceable when something goes wrong. Your desire to find new relationships rather than work at current ones may stem from not knowing enough about how to solve sexual problems.

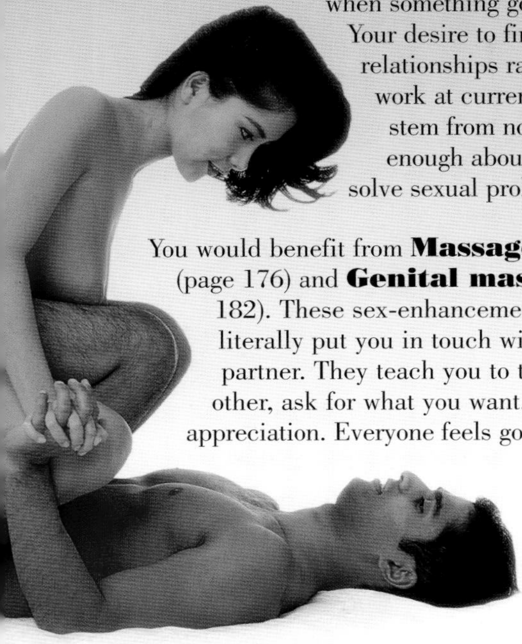

You would benefit from **Massage skills** (page 176) and **Genital massage** (page 182). These sex-enhancement exercises literally put you in touch with your partner. They teach you to talk to each other, ask for what you want, and express appreciation. Everyone feels good afterward.

Are you a **potent lover?**

Potency is about stamina, virility, and sexual health. A potent lover is one who is long-lasting (when necessary), brimming with energy, and flushed with youthful strength. Potency is a term usually applied to men and literally refers to the power of erection. However, in some contexts (such as here), it also refers to healthy, sexually interested, active females. So, are you a potent lover?

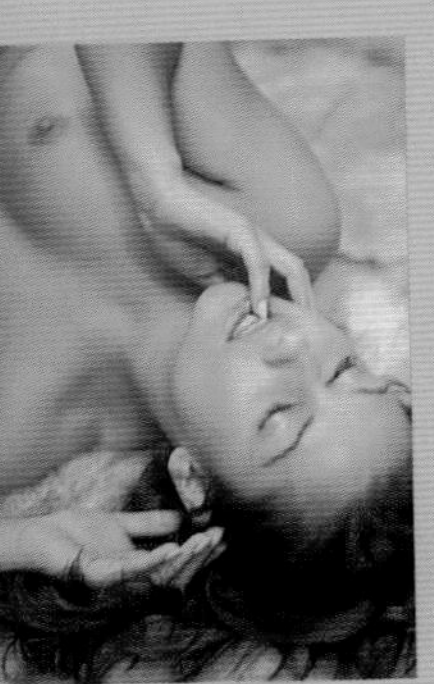

1 *Do you usually find* **you** *get* **aroused***:*

- **a** Instantly – you're ready to go with a click of your partner's fingers?
- **b** Quite easily – you need a bit of foreplay to be ready for action?
- **c** It's a struggle – you need a lot of foreplay before you feel really turned on?

2 *Do* **you** *usually* **climax***:*

- **a** Bang on time – to suit your partner?
- **b** Around the same time as your partner?
- **c** Sooner than you'd like?

3 *When bringing your* **partner** *to* **orgasm***, can you go on for hours?*

- **a** Almost always.
- **b** Most of the time.
- **c** Not as often as you'd like.

4 *When you are with a partner, do you* **like** *to have* **sex**:

a More than five times a week? ☐

b Three or four times a week? ☐

c About twice a week or less? ☐

5 *Have you ever been in a situation in which you simply* **cannot** *get* **aroused** *enough to have sex?*

a Never – you're always ready to go.

b Occasionally – when the mood hasn't been right.

c Quite a few times.

6 *Would you say that your* **sex drive** *is:*

a High – often higher than your partner's?

b Medium – that suits your partner?

c Low – can sometimes be a problem with your partner?

7 *Do you ever find sex* **painful***?*

a Never – it usually runs like clockwork.

b Sometimes – but it's not really a problem.

c Occasionally and it is offputting.

8 *Are you able to* **delay** *orgasm when the* **occasion** *demands it?*

a Yes – you can turn yourself off (and on) like a faucet.

b Sometimes – if you catch yourself early enough.

c Not as often as you'd like.

9 *Are you able to make* **love** *for as* **long** *as your partner likes?*

a Almost always – you have excellent staying power.

b Usually – but it's sometimes hard-going.

c You sometimes have to stop before your partner is ready.

10 *Are you* **comfortable** *in most sexual* **positions***?*

a Yes, you slip into them with ease.

b You find a few a little uncomfortable.

c You like to stick to the ones you know suit you.

How **potent** are you?

Mostly As – super potent

You have great all-over sexual health and are very tuned into the way your body works. You have a youthful sexual identity, which makes you spontaneous, and you enjoy variety, confident in the knowledge that you have what it takes. Please don't assume, however, that all partners are as fortunate as you. They may not be so tireless, so sexually well directed, or enjoy such brimming energy.

For the sake of your partner, I suggest you check out **Prolonging the pleasure** (page 194). Having intercourse for hours may be an interesting health workout, but it isn't always too erotic. **Masturbation during intercourse** (page 204) is another useful section if your partner needs some help keeping up with you. Super-potent lovers often worry unduly when they begin to slow down – but it is normal and natural. See **Older loving** (page 212).

Mostly Bs – potency assured

With the exception of the very young, yours is the category into which most of us fall. You are of average potency. Perhaps you experience sexual failure on occasion, but you're sensible enough to know this is normal. However, good sex is not only about virile performance. **Oral sex** (page 196) and **Genital massage** (page 182) are useful for those who are not sexual athletes.

If you are a woman who feels that her man does a poor job in sustaining intercourse, get a feel for what man-on-top intercourse feels like: get down on hands and knees

and then do "push-ups" (without moving your arms) over an imaginary lover as if having intercourse. Since the average intercourse lasts for three minutes (yes, that's all!), this is the time given for the exercise. Most women collapse after 30 seconds and suddenly appreciate their man with new enthusiasm.

Mostly Cs – reasonably potent

People with a low sex drive (many women and some men), men who suffer from premature ejaculation, and men and women who find it difficult to climax, start their sex life with natural disadvantages. Potency isn't really the issue here, although a lack of energy may be. Sex drive lies within a normal spectrum, from highly sexed through average-sexed to lower-sexed. It is normal for those who are lower-sexed to want less sex in the first place.

However, the growing number of men and women who drink and smoke to excess are finding that sex doesn't seem to work. The facts are that alcohol impairs sexual performance and smoking impairs virility. Even if you don't belong to this group, if you exercise, eat healthily, and develop your sexual technique, sex will be more sensational. See **Feeling fit for sex** (page 210).

Are you a **teasing lover?**

Some people like a partner to be sexually direct because this approach makes them feel secure. Others prefer something more provocative on the grounds that teasing is sexually challenging. Anything that challenges is going to be novel, possibly surprising, and definitely erotic, which is good for you and your relationship if you are up to it. So what sort of a lover are you?

1 *When you're out on a* **date** *with your* **partner**, *do you like to wear:*

a The sexiest, most figure-hugging ensemble in your wardrobe (and, yes, this means you men, too)? ☐

b Something revealing but not over-the-top? ☐

c Your ordinary clothes. You don't feel that you need to dress up for your partner? ☐

2 *You haven't seen your partner for a week and you know that he/she will be dying to have* **sex** *when you're* **reunited**. *Do you:*

a Spend the evening limiting your partner to kisses and caresses until he/she is chomping at the bit? ☐

b Have dinner, then get down to business? ☐

c Jump into bed at the earliest opportunity? ☐

3 *You find out your partner has a* **fetish** *about* **uniforms**. *Do you:*

a Buy the sexiest uniform outfit you can find and surprise your partner the next time you see him/her? ☐

b Dig out your old school or cheerleader's uniform for a laugh? ☐

c Think it's a bit weird? ☐

4 *When you* **undress** *before sex, do you:*

a Peel off each layer of your clothing with tantalizing eroticism? ☐

b Try to look as elegant as you can? ☐

c Rip off everything as quickly as possible? ☐

5 *When you're* **undressing** *your* **partner** *before sex, do you:*

a Take off every item slowly, with maddening languor and intensity? ☐

b Take off your partner's clothes with a little help from him/her? ☐

c Struggle with the buckles and fastenings in your haste? ☐

6 *You and your partner have just seen a movie at the cinema and agree that one* **scene** *was highly* **arousing**. *Do you:*

a Suggest you reenact the scene when you get home? ☐

b Visualize parts of the scene during sex with your partner? ☐

c Laugh and think nothing more of it? ☐

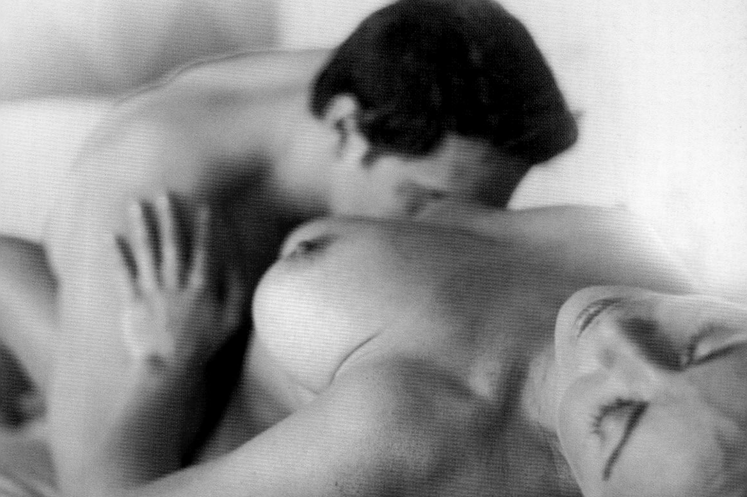

7 *When it comes to* **foreplay**, *do you:*

a Slowly play your lover's body until he/she is begging for more? ☐

b Pay attention only to your lover's genitals? ☐

c Stick to the same old routine? ☐

8 *Your partner has bought a* **sex toy** *and is aching to* **try it** *out. Do you:*

a Unwrap the toy and thrill your lover all over? ☐

b Ask your partner what he/she would like you to do with it? ☐

c Tell him/her you're not sure about sex toys? ☐

9 *When making* **love** *to your partner, do you* **like** *to:*

a Leave penetration until the point when your partner is screaming for it? ☐

b Reach penetration when you feel your partner begins to want it? ☐

c Go for penetration when you want to do so? ☐

10 *You're having sex and your partner is on the* **brink** *of* **orgasm**. *Do you:*

a Slow down in order to prolong his/her delight for as long as possible? ☐

b Maintain the same speed and tempo on the grounds that you shouldn't change what works? ☐

c Speed up so that you can reach orgasm at the same time? ☐

How **teasing** are you?

Mostly As – big tease

With a sparkle in your eye, you really know how to get your partner wound up. The way you dress and act (both in bed and out of it) are designed to keep your lover on his/her toes. You are more than willing to try out new things to spice up your sex life. Your power of delaying gratification is to be admired. You are sexually skillful and know just what to do to keep your partner begging for more.

Be aware, however, that there is a thin dividing line between teasing and tears. Be careful to read your partner accurately. Some people might get angry, others may simply turn off, lose interest, or even feel intimidated. Remember too that if you only ever tease, even this will become predictable. So use a provocative approach sparingly – you're likely to obtain better results! If you want to do a bit of advanced teasing, take a look at the **Bad slave game** (page 138) and **Listen to my tape** (page 146).

Mostly Bs – naughty but nice

You're no exhibitionist, but you keep your sexual relationship exciting and your lover has few complaints. You could be a much more erotic lover by bringing a little more teasing into the equation. Because you're a careful personality, you hesitate to do anything different when sex seems to be working well. It takes a degree of faith in one's powers of eroticism to slow sex down. The instinct is nearly always to speed it up.

Spice things up by finding out about the pyschological aspects of teasing and how to do it in **Teasing tricks** (page 152).

Then check out **Reading sexual body language** (page 220) to see if you can analyze your partner's response to your new moves.

Mostly Cs – not at ease

You are happier with the direct approach. Teasing is not right for you, and you would feel positively uneasy should you try it. There are many ways of stimulating a partner and teasing is only one of them. Talking, laughing, playing games, discussing the meaning of life are others. (One woman I know talked all the way through the sex act because she and her partner loved the idea.)

This doesn't mean you wouldn't like to bring extra eroticism into your love life. Have you ever read a sexy story out loud to your partner? Did you ever watch an erotic movie together or look at sexy photographs? These would be good ways of bringing something new to the bedroom. Or you might experiment with some of the new sex toys; they're more acceptable now than ever before.

Take a look at **Sexy photo session** (page 156) and **Sex toys** (page 160) to help you add a bit of sparkle to your sex life.

Are you a **sensual lover?**

Do you love to spend hours stroking and massaging yourself? Do you always snuggle up close to your lover's body? Do you find it difficult to tear yourself away from the slippery sensuality of his/her skin? Do food, music, and song fill you with delight? Or do you prefer to take a more cerebral approach to sex? Would you describe yourself as a sensual lover? Or not?

1 *Your lover is coming over for a* **night** *of* **passion**. *Do you:*

- **a** Prepare your bedroom with candles, perfume, and warmth?
- **b** Shake out the sheepskin rug across the living room floor?
- **c** Read aloud from a book of erotic short stories?

2 *When you sleep* **together** *do you:*

- **a** Snuggle up close all night?
- **b** Lie apart but hold hands?
- **c** Find it hard to relax next to another person?

3 *Do you keep your* **bed** *covered with:*

- **a** The silkiest, softest sheets and cushions?
- **b** Plain cotton?
- **c** Books?

4 *Your lover feels* **tense** *and uptight after a* **stressful** *day. Do you:*

a Soothingly massage him/her all over with perfumed oils and lotions? ☐

b Suggest he/she go for a walk to calm down? ☐

c Ask him/her to talk about the day? ☐

5 *Your lover* **strokes** *the side of your* **body.** *Do you feel:*

a A jolt of sexual electricity that makes you weak at the knees?

b The stirrings of something promising?

c The hand of friendship?

6 *Your lover has a gorgeous* ***derrière***. *Do you:*

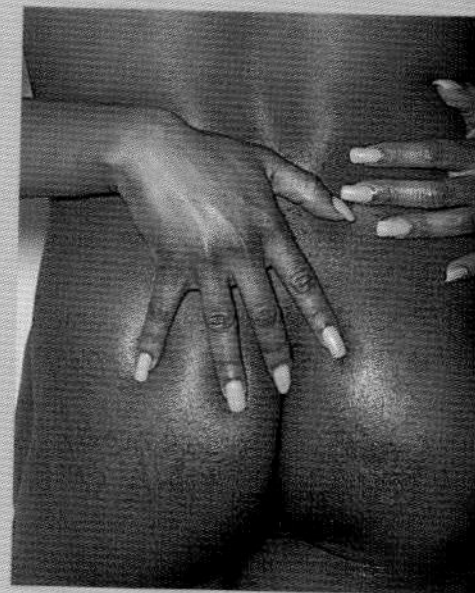

a Find it impossible to keep your hands off, even in public?

b Keep casting surreptitious glances at him/her?

c Refrain from touching but rave to your friends?

7 *When you* **kiss**, *does your partner:*

a Send out lightning bolts of sexual arousal?

b Melt in a puddle of sensual jelly?

c Pause and consider the experience?

8 *When you have* **intercourse**, *do you like to continue with* **kissing**:

a Throughout – you feel so much closer? ☐

b Sometimes – if that's what feels right for the moment? ☐

c No, on the grounds that it distracts from getting your orgasm? ☐

9 *Given a choice of* **vacation** *would you opt for:*

a A week on a Caribbean beach in a luxury vacation resort? ☐

b A week at a spa, with massage and body treatments as part of the deal? ☐

c An activity vacation, that included swimming, riding, and waterskiing? ☐

10 *You ought to get up and do any* **number** *of household* **tasks**. *Do you:*

a Snuggle up against your partner's gorgeous warm body and continue sleeping? ☐

b Rub your body so provocatively against your partner's that he/she wakes up and wants to have sex? ☐

c Promise yourself an afternoon nap and roll out of bed? ☐

How **sensual** are you?

Mostly As – scorchingly sensual

You are sensual to your very core. This means that you are both responsive and capable of inspiring incredible sexual reaction. The most sensual lovers are those who arouse a partner with the tip of a finger. You luxuriate in rubbing, stroking, hugging, and holding. Given a chance, you would actually wallow in a partner's body.

All this physicality means that you are a gorgeous person to be loved by. It seems perfectly normal and natural to you to sidle up to a lover and drape yourself all over him/her. Amazingly, not everyone likes it. It's vital to understand that other people can actually feel suffocated by so much physical display. So learn to evaluate a new partner in terms of how much closeness he/she feels comfortable with. Take a look at **Reading sexual body language** (page 220).

Mostly Bs – privately passionate

You are certainly sensual but can adjust your body language to adapt. You don't feel hurt or rejected when a partner prefers to read a book after lovemaking instead of hugging, as long as the lovemaking itself feels great. You understand that although closeness is great, sometimes so is distance. You are self-sufficient enough to enjoy time alone if there is a partner in the background.

However, you are also a little inhibited. You assume that warmth and love is to be expressed in private only and when you do find a great new partner you don't want to push your luck by being overly expressive. Perhaps you have experienced rejection in the past. You could be missing out on some physical sex activity that your body yearns for. Don't be afraid to ask for more hugs if you want them. If your inhibitions make this hard, try doing the **Yes/no exercise** (page 234).

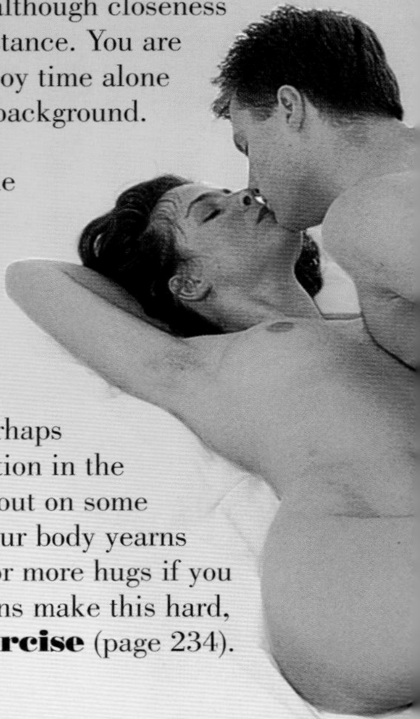

Mostly Cs – more cerebral

Of course you enjoy the sensation of good sex. But you are just as likely to get pleasure from thinking about it. Bodily sensuality isn't everything, and you are not easily distracted. If doing well at work means getting up and leaving the house promptly, you will do it – however tempting the partner you leave behind. You find so many enjoyments in life that spending huge chunks of time on mindless (but wonderful) pastimes such as massage feels inefficient. And you don't really miss touch. You get as much as you want. There is so much else to bring pleasure, such as the joy of reading.

All this is great provided you partner someone similar. But if your lover is a sensualist, you will need to see things from their point of view. Touch to a true sensualist is like food and drink. He/she must have it! See **Massage skills** (page 176), and **Genital massage** (page 182). Learning how to stimulate your partner's G-spot would also be hot! See **About the G-spot** (page 192.)

part two

gra

with dis

duating
tinction

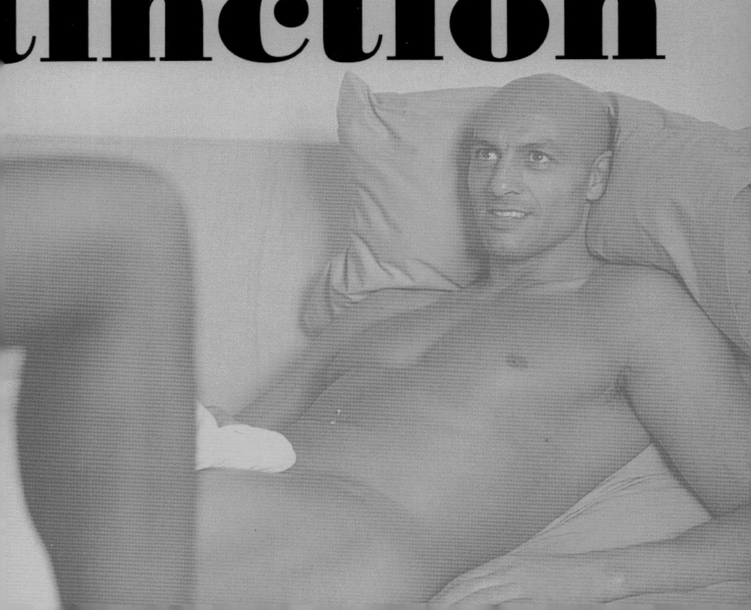

Playing by the rules

If you play any sex games, it is vital that you and your partner trust one another implicitly. For this reason, always establish some rules first. If you have any doubts, or your sex partner is a stranger, do not play.

It is also imperative to be able to stop a sex game if necessary. You cannot rely on "no" or "stop," since protest may be a part of your game. Before playing, establish a private code word between the two of you that means, without doubt, "I want to stop right now."

Moves you may not make

✘ Take the action beyond the agreed limit.
✘ Disregard the use of a partner's agreed code word.
✘ Expose a partner publicly (this includes showing photographs of your sexual activities to others).
✘ Bring in any third party unless you and your partner have talked about and agreed to this previously.
✘ Physically or emotionally hurt or damage your lover.

The sexual **initiation rites**

Want to play some sex games? You might enjoy the sexual initiation rites. You and your partner can take turns to give and receive the rites, with the recipient blindfolded throughout.

Identify the odors of sex

You are offered a variety of unusual scents and asked which you associate with what aspect of sex. Expect to be presented with anything from massage oil to perspiration, rubber, seminal fluid, or vaginal juices.

Identify tactile temptations

You are offered a variety of unusual materials or textures to identify and comment on. These might include silk, satin, fur, feathers, ice, toothpaste, or lubricating jelly.

Identify the accessories of punishment

You are subjected to being lightly spanked with a hand; caned with a lightweight bamboo; paddled with a soft suede cat o' nine tails; or stimulated with a fur mitt.

The **bad slave** game

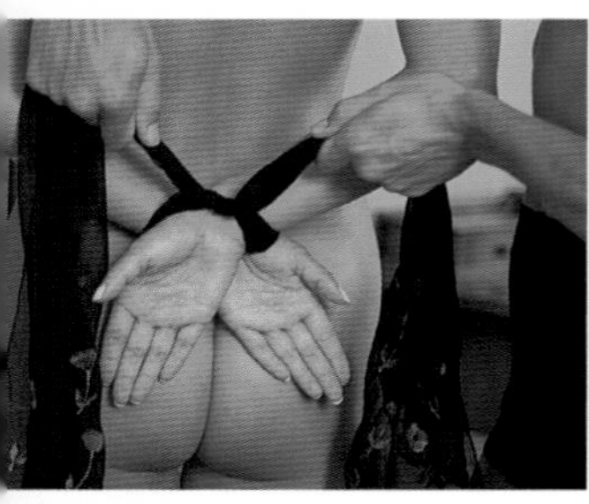

The room is dark and a single candle burns. Your partner has been a bad slave and you explain that bad slaves must always be punished for their wrongdoing.

Order her to kneel against the bed. When she does so, tie her hands with soft ties (men's ties work well), securing one to each side of the bed. Pull her arms forward as you tie her wrists so that her naked rear is exposed and her genitals are fully in view. This will make her feel more helpless and at your mercy. Then leave the room.

Time for discipline

Just when she thinks you have forgotten her, reenter the room. Discover that she has moved slightly. This is strictly forbidden, you tell her, and so you must punish her for her disobedience.

She protests, but unsuccessfully. You might punish her by rubbing her bottom first so that it gets warm, and then spanking it lightly to give her a shock.

Each time you leave and come back into the room, you discover that she has moved again – and so the punishment continues. How else can you teach this particularly bad slave a lesson? You might lightly cane her or pretend to take her by force.

Please note that exactly the same game can be played with a male partner as the slave.

Very important! Never play bondage games with a partner who seems in any way unwilling.

The **big stick**

Caning and spanking may sound painful but, for many people, a light slap of the hand or playful blow with a paddle brings the blood pleasantly to the surface, making the skin feel warm and tingly – all precursors of erotic arousal.

Safe instruments that do not hurt are carpet beaters, paddles, spatulas, whisks, and soft flails. Crops, rulers, and canes do hurt, so use them sparingly. If a partner feels real pain, call a halt.

A spanking game

- ♥ You ask, "where would you like it? Here or there?" When your partner says "here," then spank or cane somewhere else.
- ♥ When your partner protests, then do it somewhere else. The idea of the game is to tease and tantalize.

Warning! Agree on a safety code word first. There must be a way in which a partner can end the session.

Dressing up for sex

Wearing something unexpected has the erotic power to shock – pleasantly! If you tell each other your fantasies, add realism to the conversation by dressing the part. Don't be afraid to experiment with cosmetics – and guys, this includes you!

Throw a fancy dress party

Send out party invitations stating the condition of entry: guests must be dressed in outfits that reflect their favorite sexual fetishes or fantasies.

- ♥ Tight, short leather – or anything made of leather – has sadomasochistic overtones.
- ♥ Fake fur suggests decadence, especially if you are naked beneath a fake fur coat.
- ♥ Uniforms – especially those associated with figures of authority – are always sexy. Dress up as a fire fighter, police officer, doctor, nurse, or schoolteacher. Servant and schoolgirl outfits suggest servility and innocence.
- ♥ Cross-dressing can be highly erotic. Try to create at least a moment's uncertainty as to your true gender.

Birthday treats

Adopt the idea of playing a sex game on your birthday. You might:

- ♥ Go to a party dressed as the opposite sex.
- ♥ Make love dressed as the opposite sex. You might even use a strap-on dildo to keep in role!
- ♥ Give each other a sensual bath and indulge yourselves by feeding one another with exotic prepared fruits and flutes of champagne.
- ♥ Pretend that you are sex toy testers and work your way through an entire range.

And when it's all over? Well, naturally, you cut the birthday cake.

Listen to my tape

The aim of this game is to record yourself on tape expressing the most suggestive, lecherous, arousing ideas you can think of, and describing the marvelous plans you have for lovemaking with your partner.

You might record an erotic short story or two, S&M commands, or an endless list of sexual praise. You could use the tape:

On your own

If you cannot see each other for awhile, you can listen to the tape instead. Perhaps you can carry out some of the verbal suggestions in private.

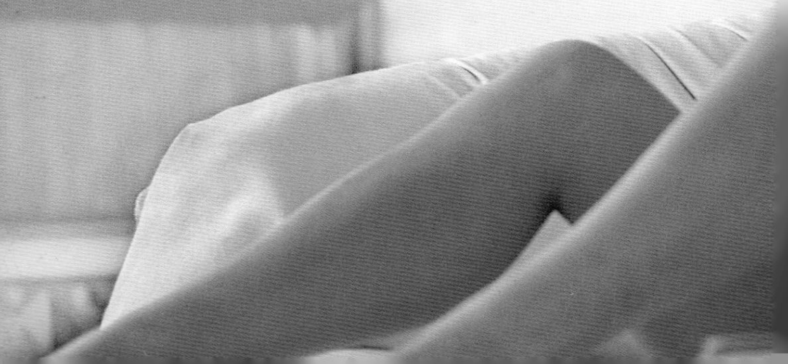

As a tease

You could incorporate the tape into a game of sexual imagination. You might blindfold your partner and play the tape in the pretence there is someone else in the room with sexual intention. You could also force your partner to listen to the tape while you are in the next room. How could this work? By eventually making the partner angry? Well, anger itself is a state of emotional arousal and can be used (provided it hasn't been allowed to go on too long) as another route into exciting lovemaking.

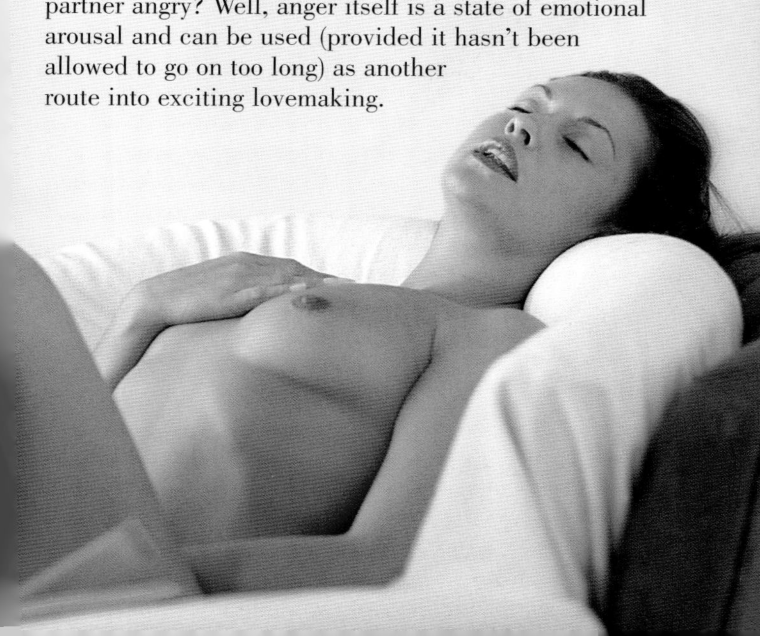

Fun sex positions

Lyons stagecoach

The woman sits on her man's penis with her legs toward his shoulders while she leans back on her hands.

Horse of Hector

Her knees are on either side of him facing toward his head. She sits up and leans back during penetration and he may raise his knees to give support. Good for deep penetration.

Back to front

He lies on his back, with his knees raised (as shown). She sits astride him upon his penis, facing toward his feet and leaning forward against his thighs and knees.

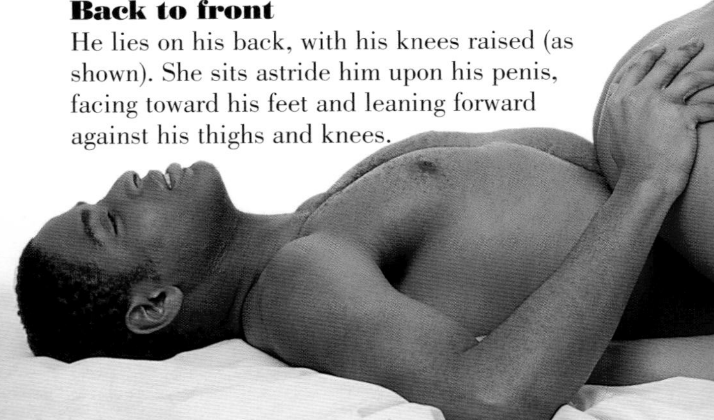

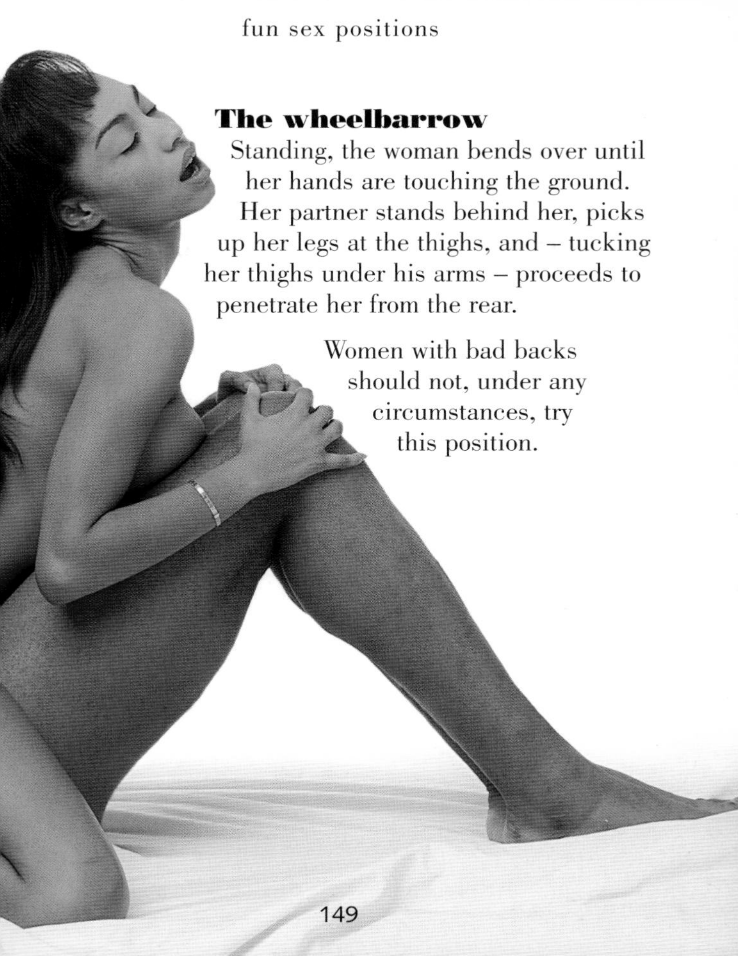

The wheelbarrow

Standing, the woman bends over until her hands are touching the ground. Her partner stands behind her, picks up her legs at the thighs, and – tucking her thighs under his arms – proceeds to penetrate her from the rear.

Women with bad backs should not, under any circumstances, try this position.

A sexual **banquet**

Plan to relax and pamper your lover for hors-d'oeuvres – it's the best way to whet his or her sexual appetite.

Feast the senses

- ♥ Prepare a warm, sweetly scented bath for your lover. As he/she sits back in the water, pour champagne into a fluted glass and serve. Feed him/her from a platter of beautifully prepared exotic fruit.
- ♥ Climb into the bath so that you are sitting behind your lover and cradle him/her in your arms. If you feel like pouring champagne down each other, fine.
- ♥ When you emerge from the bath, wrap your lover in warm, fluffy towels (prepared earlier) and don't let him/her do any of the drying him/herself.

The food of love

- ♥ Now use food to stimulate your partner's body. Smear honey on the skin and lick it off. Adorn him/her with dabs of cream and feast on it. Run an ice-cube over the nipples, lick chocolate sauce from the neck.

♥ As he/she begins to get aroused, dribble a little champagne onto the genitals and lick it off. You might even place a bagel around his penis and nibble on it, "accidentally" nibbling on him a little, too. Have fun.

Teasing tricks

- ♥ Leave on a few clothes instead of stripping naked.
- ♥ Women: certain clothes (such as suspender belts and stockings) are extremely provocative. Men: leaving your socks on is not.
- ♥ Suggest one sexual activity, then do another.
- ♥ In sex games, put your partner into a double bind. If he/she is disobedient, tell your partner he/she will have to be punished. Then make it impossible for him/her to be obedient.
- ♥ Make punishment a combination of warm stroking then firm spanking. Lull him/her into a false security with the stroking even though he/she knows your hand may fall at any minute.
- ♥ If your partner is very turned on, deliberately withhold arousal for a while.

Sexy love notes

The whole point of a love note is to remind the other person of your existence and to show them that you care. The best way to do this is to catch their attention with something that excites, intrigues, or stimulates.

You might manage this by making them laugh, wonder, or by directly turning them on. Remember that if you do make a sexual, or any other, promise in your love note, it is very important that you fulfil it!

You might:

♥ Send an invitation that reads: "Esmeralda Diamond requests your company at a banquet. Main course – Esmeralda Diamond."

♥ Tuck a note under the windshield wiper on your partner's car that says, "Nice car. How about a rally?"

- Send half a photograph – the top half – accompanied by a note that says, "If you would like to know what is on the other half, meet me at such and such."
- Write a note in the shape of a classified ad, saying, "Young hooker needs rescuing. If you think you might be able to prevent me from walking the streets, meet me at Johnny's Bar." Follow this up by dressing the part and waiting at a bar that has some kind of a sexual reputation. Then act in character when your partner turns up.
- Or, if you are a man: "Young transvestite urgently seeks moral reformer. Meet me at Madame Fifi's." Dress up in full drag and don't forget the eye shadow. Then act the part!

Sexy photo session

A camera can capture certain erotic moments. If you want a visible memory of your half-naked partner looking at you with unashamed desire, the next best thing to reality is to keep a celluloid copy in your wallet.

One woman sent her man a series of gorgeous snapshots (taken with a time-release mechanism) in which she posed as:

- ♥ An old-fashioned movie star
- ♥ A dominatrix complete with whip and thigh-high shiny boots
- ♥ A dish at a banquet
- ♥ A sultry harem girl.

Erotic tip Assess your partner's taste. Go for what pleases him/her rather than what pleases you.

Shower power

A shower combines heat, pressure, moisture, and friction all in one device, making it a perfect sex toy. According to *The Hite Report*, many women's favorite method of reaching orgasm is to use the shower to give themselves a water massage.

Shower games

- ♥ Cover one another in liquid soap and give each other an erotic massage in the shower.
- ♥ Use the shower to give either pleasure or punishment alternately. To give pleasure, direct warm water at the genitals. As punishment, give a blast of cold water on the back.
- ♥ See how much you can excite each other using only the jets of water from the showerhead.
- ♥ Surprise your partner with some impromptu sex in the shower.

The best position for shower sex (or the one in which you are both least likely to slide off the shower tray!) is where the woman bends over and the man penetrates her from behind.

Sex **toys**

Erotic toys can add novelty and excitement to your sex life. There are all kinds of toys to suit every taste, so why not get together with your partner and write a saucy shopping list ...

Vibrators

♥ You can buy silent vibrators designed to fit inside the palm of the hand – the sort of equipment your maiden aunt would never recognize.

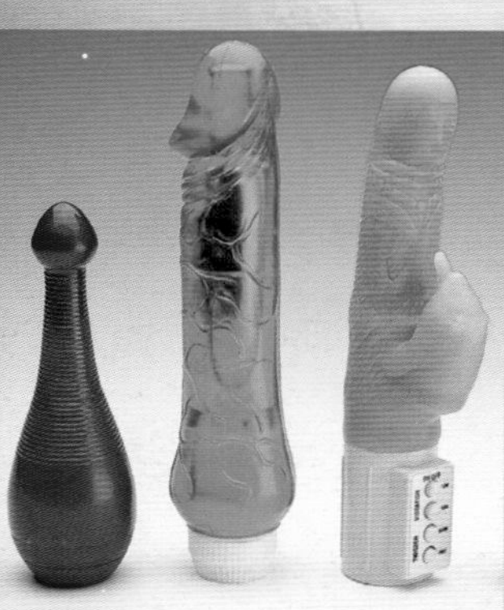

♥ You can buy vibrators made of glowing jelly-like substances in jewel-bright colors.

♥ Many cock rings now vibrate – they are powered by a tiny battery.

♥ Some cock rings incorporate special probes that stimulate the G-spot or the prostate gland; others have special clitoral probes situated on the front.

♥ One new vibrator is a tiny finger probe, so small as to be virtually undetectable. It is powered by a tiny silver bullet battery and can wreak havoc under the table at dinner parties.

Bondage wrap

This is a version of cling wrap that comes in sinister black, scarlet hussy red, or fleshy pink. It's fun as part of bondage games. It also looks spectacular and, with a bit of imagination, can be worn as a fashion accessory. Of course, simple cling wrap can be just as exciting.

Sex swing

Invented by an enterprising couple (who themselves feature on their instructional video), this is a system of seats and straps hanging from a central fastening. The idea is that the person on the swing is easily available to a partner who likes his/her lover passive. It also has the advantage of being practical if you are unlucky enough to suffer from arthritic joint problems.

Weekend break

Want to relieve the gloom of winter or celebrate the renewal of spring? One way to liven up your sex life is to whisk your partner away for a weekend break. Since novelty is one factor that makes the early days of a sexual relationship so exciting, it's a shame that more of us don't go away together far more often. Weekends somewhere other than home are the antidote to sexual routine and, dare I say it, sexual boredom.

Whether you stay at a lovely country house hotel with roaring log fires or borrow a friend's apartment for the weekend, it's the change of routine that's so great.

Think about long, relaxed walks during the day, early suppers, and then retiring early to the bedroom. Or the living room. Or anywhere else that is handy. You might give each other a warm bath, make a special surprise of giving small gifts, plan a wonderful massage. Then see what happens afterward!

The **map test** game

Everyone's sensual areas differ. A sensual site on one body will not necessarily be the same on another individual. This is why it is important you build up a mental map of your partner's personal erogenous zones. How can you do this? By playing the following game.

How to play

- ♥ One partner sits or lays down nude. The other gently strokes a 2-in (5-cm) area of the skin and asks the partner to rate the sensation on a scale of plus to minus 3.
- ♥ If the touch feels great, it is rated plus 3. If it doesn't feel particularly special, the score is 0, and if it feels unpleasant, anything on the minus scale. This way you can quite quickly find out which areas of the skin feel sensational and which don't.

- The principal zones are the lips and eyelids, ears, shoulders, breasts and nipples, and, of course, the genitals.
- Many people also find that having the feet stroked is surprisingly arousing. But there are other areas full of surprises – try stroking down the sides of the breasts, for example.

When lovemaking later on, build on your newfound knowledge and stimulate the newly discovered hot spots.

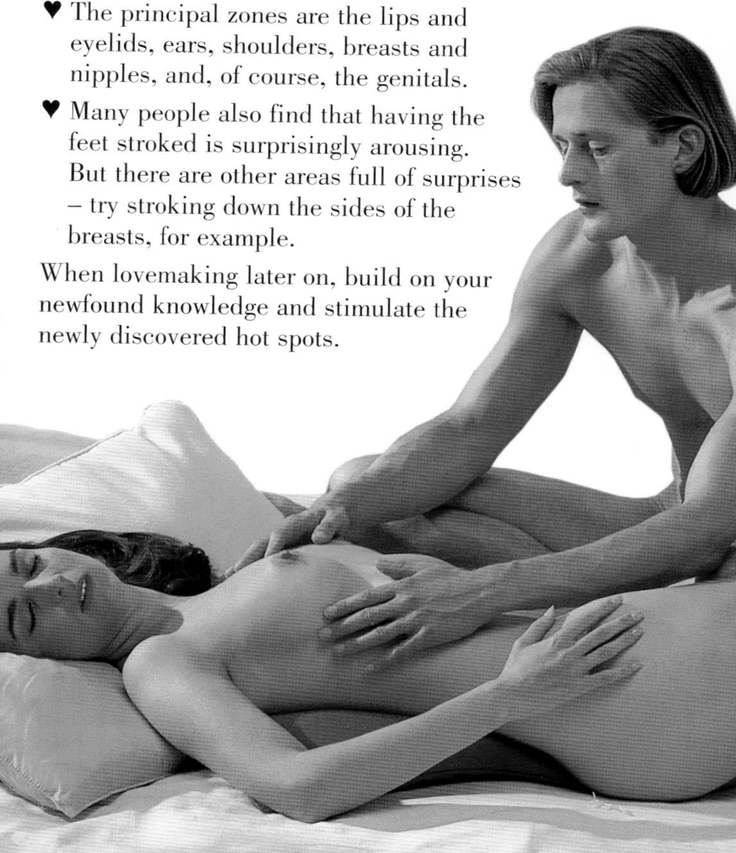

Thrilling your partner

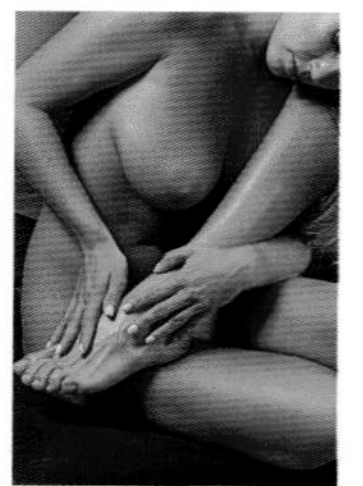

All relationships benefit from the element of surprise. One way of pleasantly thrilling a partner is to treat them to an unexpected erotic experience they've never had before …

The pampered foot

At first glance, this may not seem too erotic. But that is probably because you have never experienced it. If you wash your partner's feet in warm water, dry them with warm fluffy towels, and then proceed to massage every square inch with a peppermint massage lotion, he/she will truly thank you.

Erotic tip! Pull your finger very slowly backward and forward between the toes.

The mink coat meeting

There's nothing like an element of real risk to get the heart thudding. If you've never tried it once in your lifetime, you might think about the experiment of walking along the street, wearing nothing but a fur coat, knowing that your lover waits for you at the end of your journey. It's scary – and amazing.

A vibrator extraordinaire

Whether you are new to vibrators or have used them before, think about investing in a model that is a bit different. If, for example, he has never experienced an anal pulsator, take the plunge. If she has never had her G-spot stimulated, there's a vibrator designed to stretch right inside. Take a look at a good sex toy website and choose what would be good for you.

Did you **know...?**

Why not test your general sexual knowledge to find out whether you know as much as you think you do ... for example, did you know that:

- ♥ When they orgasm, men and women experience contractions at the same rate (every 0.8 seconds)?
- ♥ Some people say the G-spot doesn't really exist?
- ♥ The clitoris and labia have a form of erection just as the penis does?
- ♥ The prostate gland, inside the male rectum, can bring a man to orgasm through steady pressure being applied, sometimes without him even getting an erection?
- ♥ In the womb the human fetus is female for the first six weeks even if it eventually develops into a boy?
- ♥ The younger you are when you first have sex, the more prone you are to genital infections?
- ♥ The hormone testosterone is now thought to be responsible for sexual desire, sensitivity, and performance in both sexes?
- ♥ You can experience orgasm in any site of the body?

Safer sex

By practicing safer sex, you can significantly reduce the risk of contracting a range of sexually transmitted diseases (STDs), including HIV (human immunodeficiency virus) and AIDS (acquired immune deficiency syndrome).

When a man's penis penetrates a woman's vagina during unprotected intercourse, she is exposed to his semen and he is exposed to her vaginal fluids. Since viruses and other infections can be transmitted in these fluids, this is a potentially risky activity. Safer sex is sexual activity that does not involve any exchange of bodily fluids and so helps protect you against diseases.

Anyone who has concerns or doubts about the sexual health or history of a partner should practice safer sex. Only if you have a clean bill of

sexual health and have sex only with each other, are you safeguarded.

The principles of safer sex

- ♥ Use a condom during any kind of penetrative sex.
- ♥ Have non-penetrative sex. Activities such as caressing and massage are all low-risk. Try mutual masturbation or oral sex using a condom.
- ♥ Avoid sex with anyone who has open sores on the genitals.

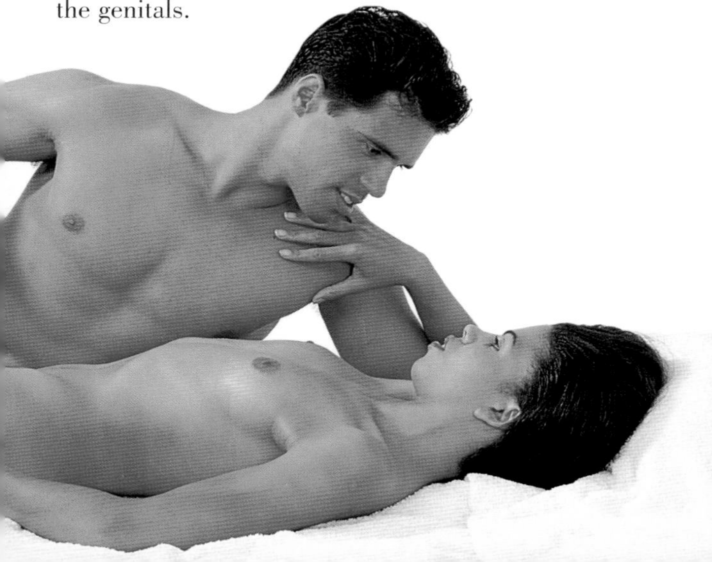

Condom know-how

The condom is not only an effective form of contraception, but it also acts as a barrier to infection. Putting on a condom correctly can sometimes make the difference between safety and sickness.

Using condoms safely

- ♥ Start with a genital massage.
- ♥ Turn the massage into masturbation as a preliminary to fitting the condom.
- ♥ When fitting the sheath, make sure you squeeze all the air out of the tip using your thumb and forefinger – even a tiny air bubble could cause the condom to split during intercourse.
- ♥ While squeezing the tip, put the sheath on the head of his penis and, with your other hand, roll it down to the base of the foreskin.

- When he withdraws after sex, make sure that she holds the condom in place to prevent it from slipping into the vagina and possibly expeling semen.
- Condoms can also be used to make oral sex safer – though it might be an idea to use flavored varieties.

Kissing skills

Ancient erotic classic the *Kama Sutra* reckoned that kissing was an important part of loving and listed over a dozen different types of embrace.

Here are just a few of the kisses it recommends:

The Bent Kiss

When the heads of two lovers are bent toward each other and kissing happens at an angle (as shown below).

The Turned Kiss
When one lover turns the face of the other by holding the head and chin, and then kissing (as shown right).

The Straight Kiss
This refers to lips on lips – the kind of kiss that marks the beginning of a relationship.

The Pressed Kiss
Where the lower lip is pressed with much force, either by your lips alone or while being held and kissed simultaneously.

The Clasping Kiss
When you take both the lips of the other, between your own. Not practical if the man has a moustache!

Massage skills

Sensual massage needs to be carried out in comfortable, sweet-smelling surroundings. Heat is essential since if cold air hits the skin, the skin tenses and touch is felt as painful rather than pleasurable.

Golden rules

- ♥ Massage should be done on thick toweling on the floor rather than on a bed – a bed is too "bouncy."
- ♥ Massage needs privacy so that you feel secure. If there are other people in the house, it's

wise to lock the door so that neither of you fears interruption.

- ♥ Clean, warm hands are essential. Even a speck of dirt can feel like a pinprick traveling across the skin. Make sure your partner's skin doesn't tense at first touch by heating the massage oil so that it is warm, but not hot (try floating the bottle in the bath). Warm your hands, too.
- ♥ Remove all jewelry that is likely to catch, such as rings and watches.
- ♥ Always partially rub massage oil into your own hands before applying it. Never drop oil onto your partner's body because he/she will feel it as a huge shock.
- ♥ Once the body is oiled, and the massage begins, do not remove both hands at the same time until the massage is ended, not even when you need more oil.
- ♥ Try to maintain a leisurely, even rhythm as you massage – don't speed it up; keep it slow!

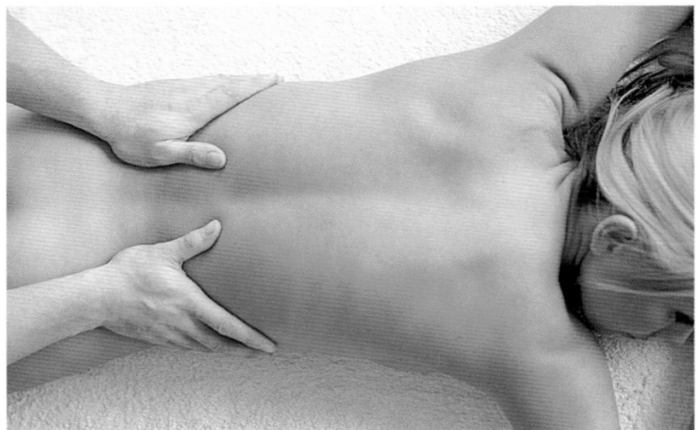

Circling

This is the basic and most useful massage stroke.

- ♥ Using both hands, palms down, circle on your partner's skin. Always circle away from the spine and don't circle on any bony areas.
- ♥ You can use the whole hand to circle, using either a firm or a light pressure, or you can circle with the fingertips or even with the fingernails (nails feel incredibly arousing).
- ♥ It's good to start off with firm strokes and then lighten up as your partner relaxes. Always massage slowly.

The Glide

This is the most spectacular movement in any massage and is used on the back only.

- Your partner lies facedown. You sit on his/her upper thighs. Place your hand on the lowest part of your partner's bottom with palms flat and the fingers pointing toward the head.
- Lean on your hands so that the weight of your body pushes your hands up and along the back toward the head. Don't force the movement – let it take as long as necessary. When you reach the neck, bring your hands around the shoulders, down the arms and back to the lower buttocks again.
- Repeat twice.

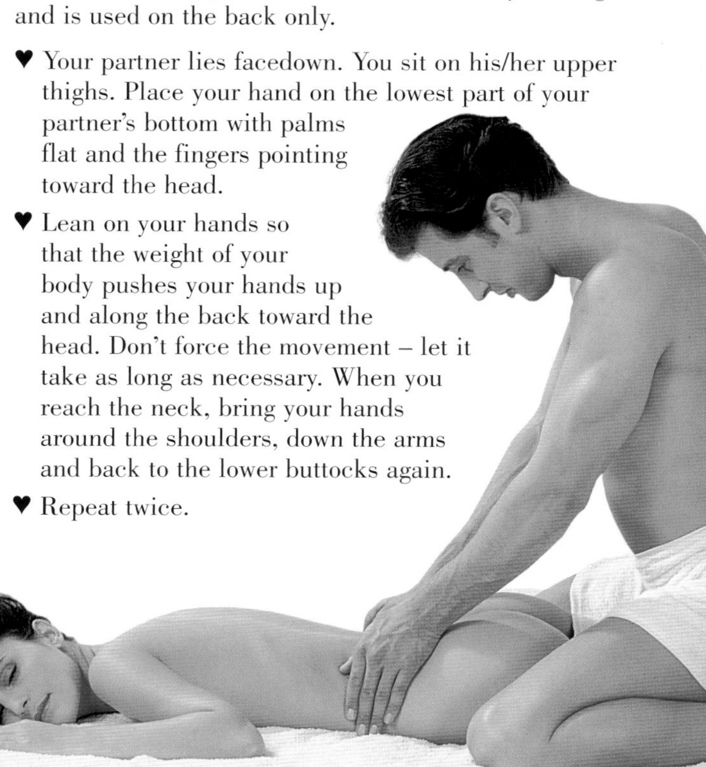

Weighting

This massages the stress away from the lower back and is great for the spine, which takes a lot of stress from holding the body upright all day.

- ♥ Sitting to one side of your partner, place your hands on either side of the spine, just below the waistline, heel of the hand to the spine, fingers toward the floor.
- ♥ Lean heavily on your hands and allow the force of your body to move your hands apart and down toward the hips, then the ground, as slowly as possible.
- ♥ Repeat the same movement a couple of times, moving from the waist, down to the area just above the tail of the spine.

If you want to pay some attention to the arms and legs, hand over hand pulling strokes work well on the limbs.

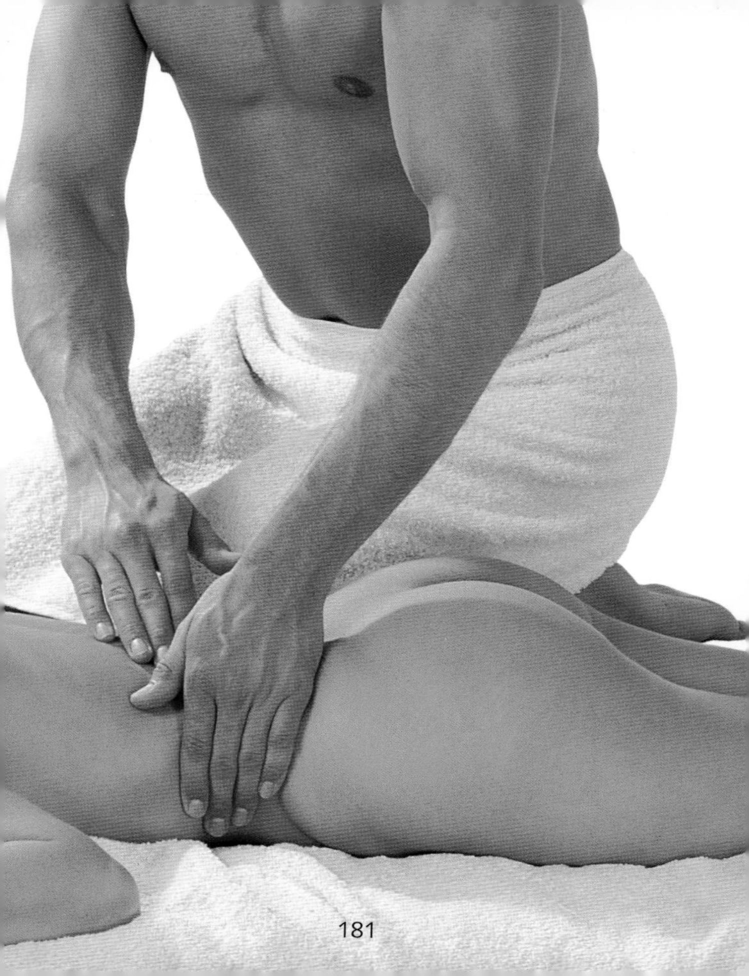

Genital **massage**

A genital massage should always follow a whole-body massage to ensure your partner is fully relaxed.

For her

Clitoral maneuvers

Extremely delicately, making sure your touch is almost featherlight and using plenty of lubrication, run your finger first around the head and then up and down the shaft of her clitoris.

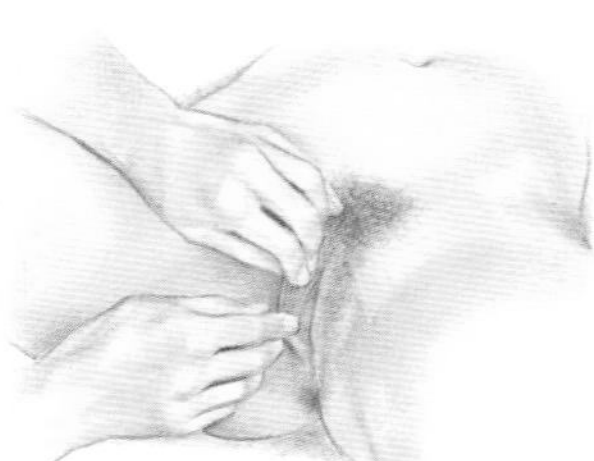

Wibbling

Start with one of the outer labia. Using both your hands at the same time, gently pull on it, then let go, just as you might do if this were the bottom lip of your mouth.

Gentle hair tease

With both hands, take tiny tufts of pubic hair and tug gently. Cover the entire pubic area. This gives exquisite prickling sensations.

Duck's bill

Position one hand into a duck's bill shape and angle it so that the bill is directed at her clitoris. With the other hand, gently pour the warmed (not hot) oil over your hands so that it slowly streams onto her genitals – producing a kind of warm flooding sensation.

For him

The corkscrew

Hold the shaft of the penis in both hands, pointed in the same direction. Twist the hands in opposite directions to each other, then bring them back, then twist again.

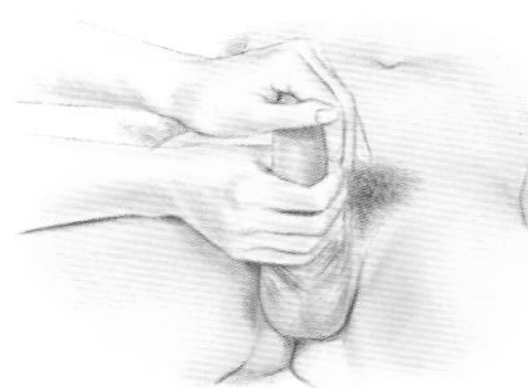

The lemon squeezer

Steady the penis by grasping it around the middle with one hand. Rub the cupped lubricated palm of your other hand around the head of the penis, as if you were juicing a lemon. As you do this, start pulling the steadying hand up and down the penis so there are two actions happening simultaneously.

The countdown

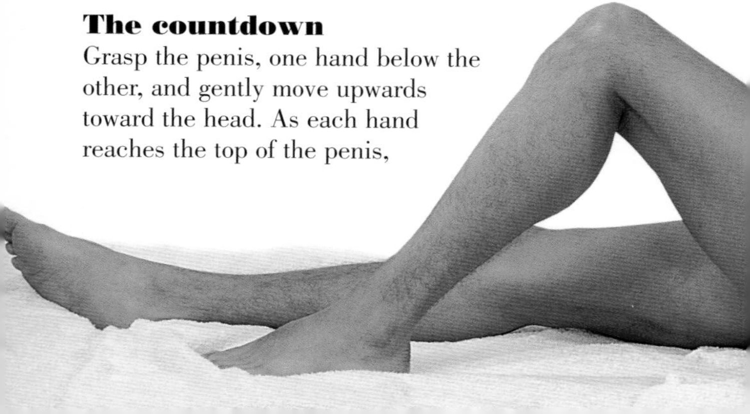

Grasp the penis, one hand below the other, and gently move upwards toward the head. As each hand reaches the top of the penis, take it back again to the base (without touching) and then repeat the stroke. After nine upward strokes, reverse the direction so that this time you are making downward strokes (nine of them). Next do eight of each direction, then seven, then six, and so on down to one.

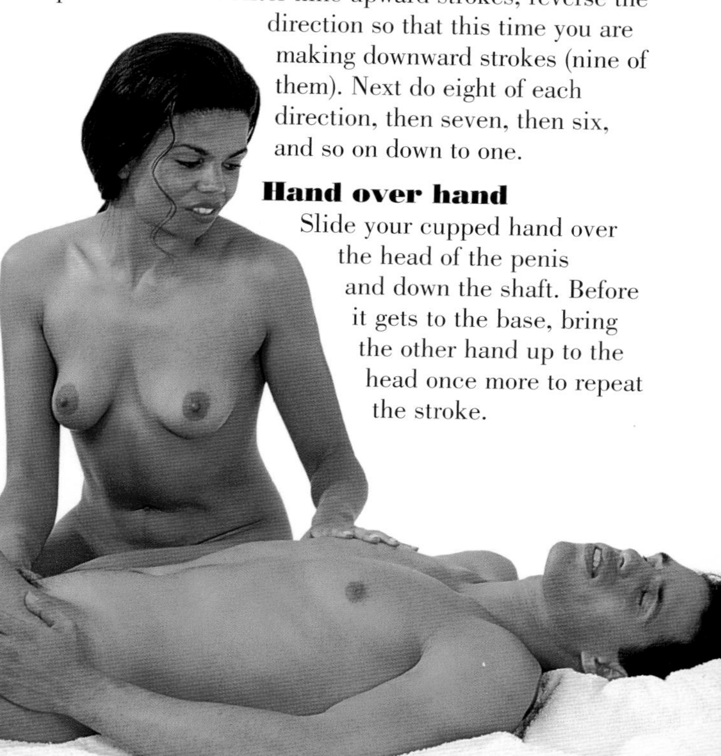

Hand over hand

Slide your cupped hand over the head of the penis and down the shaft. Before it gets to the base, bring the other hand up to the head once more to repeat the stroke.

Three-handed massage

Men, start by giving your lover a back massage and bring your legs across her thighs so that you are sitting astride her. Lavishly oil not only her buttocks but also your own abdomen, genitals, and thighs.

♥ Without interrupting your sensual massage of her back, let your well-oiled lower half glide backward and forward over her thighs and buttocks so that your genitals are in contact with her skin and effectively massaging her as well.

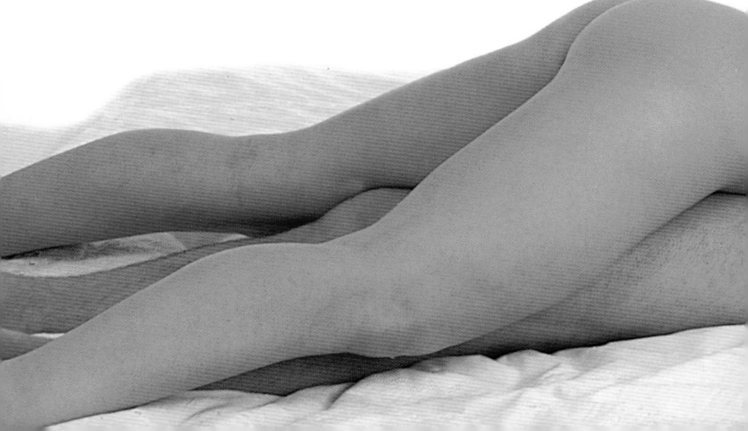

♥ As you continue, let your penis find its slippery way between her slightly parted legs and make its own contact with her vagina. Penetrate her exceptionally slowly and let your hands massage at the same time so that all the movements blend.

Women, you may be able to manage the female equivalent of the three-handed massage by giving him a front massage and using your whole body to slide over him.

Soapsud massage

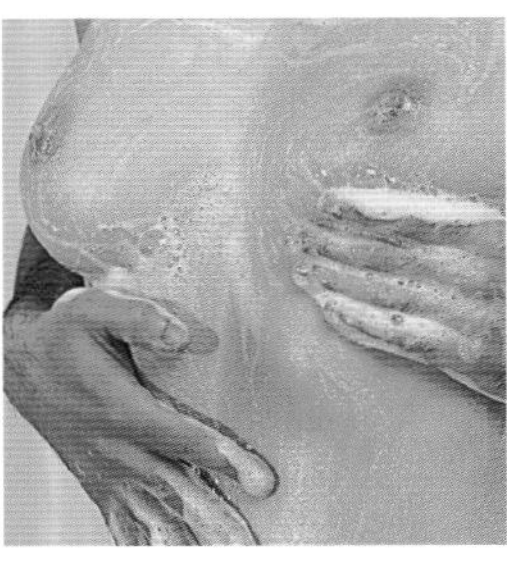

- ♥ Enjoy a warm shower or a warm bath together so that the two of you feel relaxed and clean.
- ♥ Lay down double towels on the floor (preferably on the bathroom floor) and put your partner, stomach down, on top of them.
- ♥ Using a liquid foaming soap, coat both your partner's back and your front liberally – so much foam that you can hardly see the skin.
- ♥ Then lie facedown on your partner's back and wriggle, slide, and body surf across his/her back.

Warning! Don't do this if your partner is much smaller than you – you do not want to crush his/her body.

Clitoral stimulation

The clitoris is a tiny button at the top of the vagina, just underneath the pubic mound. It acts much like a receiver and transmitter of wonderful sexy sensations.

If you pay attention to the clitoris by stroking it in certain ways, the clitoris sends messages to the brain. The brain then says to itself, "this is great!" and sends back messages to the clitoris and genitals telling them to get aroused.

The more sensation the woman receives, the greater the build-up of sexual tension – until eventually (hopefully) climax dispels the tension and her body state returns to normal.

Clitoral strokes

♥ Practice a short up-and-down stroke on the left-hand side of the clitoris, then on the right-hand side.

♥ Practice a light stroke, then a hard stroke.

♥ Try twirling directly on the clitoral head.

- Then try twirling around the clitoral head.
- Pull upward from below on the clitoris – the feeling will be sensational for your partner.

About the G-spot

The G-spot is the name for the fleshy bump located inside the vagina that, when pressed, often triggers orgasm. For some women, this G-Spot orgasm also triggers a type of ejaculation in the shape of a thin arc of

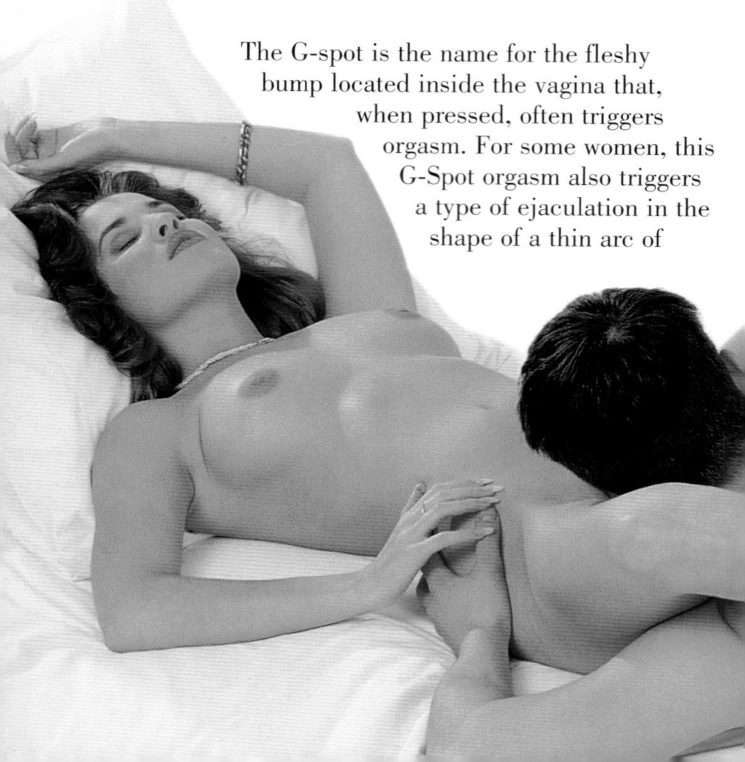

fluid from the urethra. Analysis of this liquid has shown that it is very similar to seminal fluid except, of course, it doesn't contain sperm.

However, to complicate things, not every woman appears to possess a G-spot, nobody quite knows what it is, very few women "ejaculate," and some people contend that there isn't any such thing at all.

How to find the G-spot

If you want to locate your G-spot, it's best to ask your lover to help you rather than try to find it yourself. This is because this sensitive spot tends to be located so far back along the vagina that only the very longest fingers have a chance of reaching it. It is situated at the far end of the anterior wall (or the upper wall) of the vagina.

- ♥ Rubbing the G-spot does not seem to produce orgasm as easily as giving it a firm, constant pressure.
- ♥ Some new vibrators are now designed with special G-spot probes that pulsate rather than vibrate – exactly what is needed.

Warning! Don't get upset if you can't find your G-spot. Not all women possess one.

Prolonging the pleasure

Sexual intercourse lasts for an average of three minutes. Unfortunately, women need far longer and far greater stimulation than this in order to climax. Unlike men! It is absolutely vital, therefore, that intercourse is seen as just the last part of the extremely pleasurable overall experience of kissing, cuddling, stroking, caressing, whispering words of excitement, mutual masturbation, and oral sex.

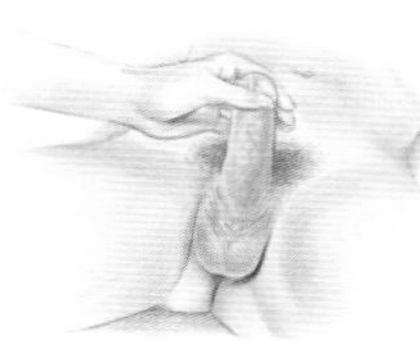

Lasting longer

If a man cannot prevent himself from ejaculating quickly, he could try the "squeeze" technique. This involves squeezing the penis hard between finger and thumb on the coronal ridge (around the head), so that you literally block the ejaculation. Although you may temporarily lose your erection, you should be able to regain it quickly. You can actually train yourself to last longer this way by practicing privately on yourself. (See also **Slowing him down**, page 206.)

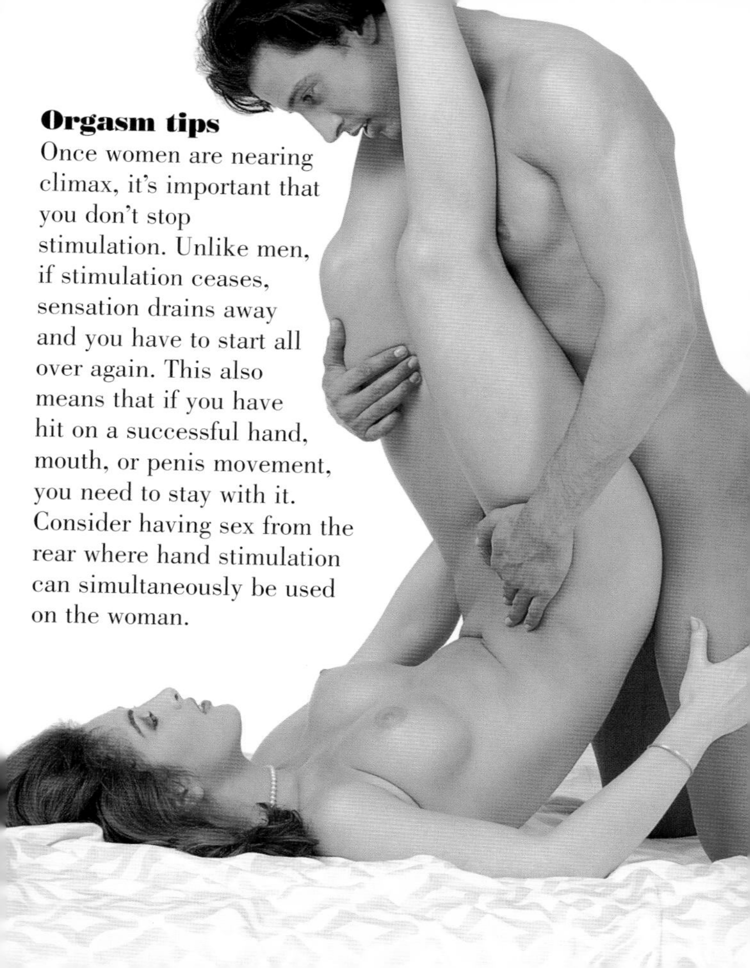

Orgasm tips

Once women are nearing climax, it's important that you don't stop stimulation. Unlike men, if stimulation ceases, sensation drains away and you have to start all over again. This also means that if you have hit on a successful hand, mouth, or penis movement, you need to stay with it. Consider having sex from the rear where hand stimulation can simultaneously be used on the woman.

Oral sex

The mouth and tongue are probably the world's greatest sex aids. The secret to good oral sex is to make him feel truly engulfed and for her to feel a gorgeous variation of sensation directly onto the clitoris.

Oral moves for her

Another secret to good oral sex is that women usually have more sensation on one side of the clitoris than the other. Respected US sex therapists Steve and Vera Bodansky insist that the left side is better!

- ♥ Position your head between and slightly below her thighs so that you can stroke your tongue upward against the shaft of her clitoris. This upward movement is the key to better clitoral sensation.
- ♥ Occasionally run your tongue over her clitoris.
- ♥ Use your tongue in different ways: curl it, flick it, use the blade, and then the tip.
- ♥ Touch her G-spot with your fingers as you lick her clitoris.
- ♥ Featherlight tongue-twirling on the top of the clitoris can be fantastic.

Advanced moves for her

Once you have tantalized her into total helplessness, try gently covering the clitoris with your mouth and flicking your tongue across it at the same time.

- ♥ If your tongue gets tired, let your fingers take over for awhile. Varying the sensation in this way can feel fantastic for her.
- ♥ Let her direct your head with her hands.
- ♥ For a really turbo-charged experience, try massaging her vaginal entrance with a vibrator as you caress her clitoris with your tongue.
- ♥ Once you've gotten into a rhythm that you know she likes, don't stop, don't slow down, and don't change the pressure. Keep going until she climaxes.

Oral moves for him

Don't wait until your man has an erection; take him into your mouth while he is still soft and partially suck on him, partially swallow. If you do this rhythmically his erection will take shape.

Tongue shaping

Holding his penis at the base with one hand, run your pointed tongue up one side of his penis, across the top and, when you go down the far side, let the underneath of your tongue take the strain. Do this two or three times before going on to use your tongue like a sculpting tool, literally licking his penis into shape.

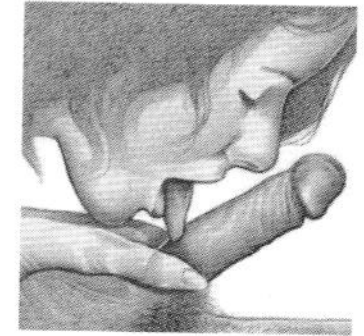

Running around in circles

Now push your mouth down on his penis so that it begins to penetrate farther into your mouth and then retreat again. As you do this, setting up a rhythm, circle your tongue around and around the head of his penis, so that it is subjected to two separate strokes and counter-rhythms at the same time. This will feel amazing for him.

Advanced moves for him

The following are seriously sensational mouth strokes.

Twanging the guitar

As you hold his penis in your mouth, flick your pointed tongue backward and forward across the top of his penis along the frenulum (the long ridge that runs the length of his penis). It's a bit like twanging a guitar string. When you feel he's enjoyed enough flicking, try humming. The humming vibrates his entire penis, and every time you change the tone of the hum, he experiences it differently.

The extended mouth

This is a good maneuver for women with small mouths. Once the head of his penis is in your mouth, place your wet hand around his penis and up against your lips so that it feels to him as if your lips have extended and completely enclosed his penis. As your mouth goes up and down on his penis, move your hand with it.

Varying the pressure

Your finger and thumb will naturally meet around his penis and you might try varying the pressure. Older men often need a much greater pressure to get any distinct sensation, while younger men simply enjoy the contrast. Don't be afraid to squeeze quite hard.

Valuing **masturbation**

It's strange to think that only 30 years ago masturbation was thought to be "wrong" or somehow immature. These days most of us think of masturbation as a perfectly normal and highly enjoyable experience – one of those God-given experiences to make life wonderful. In fact, masturbation has many values.

It is good in its own right. It is capable of providing us with a type of physical ecstasy. And if orgasm through self-stimulation has not yet been that profound, you might need to draw it out more and stimulate your whole body as well as your genitals. The more drawn out sexual pleasure becomes, the more wonderful the experience.

Masturbation allows us to get to know our own sexual response pattern. This is important because once we have such information, we are then in a position to

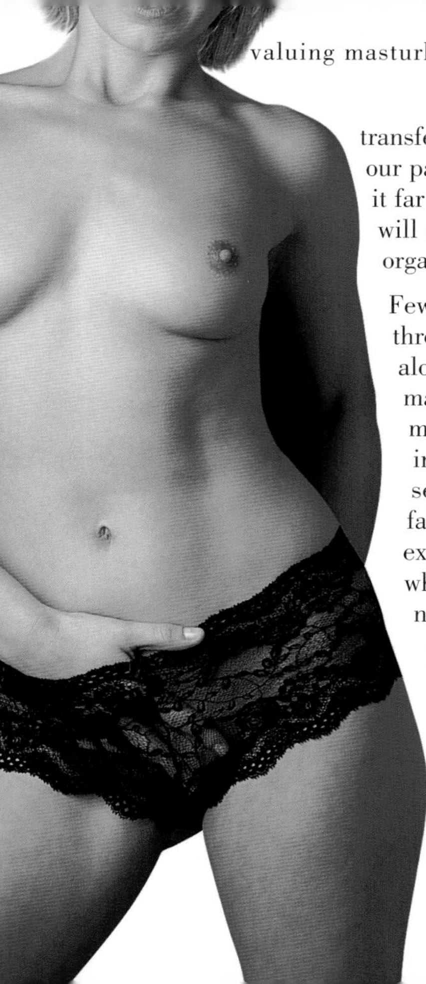

transfer the knowledge to our partner – thus making it far more likely that we will enjoy a wonderful orgasmic relationship.

Few women can climax through intercourse alone – only 30 percent manage it. By making masturbation part of intercourse, both sexes can share fabulous sexual experiences even when orgasm does not come easily.

People who don't have a sex partner still feel sexual in their own right. Thanks to self-stimulation, they can enjoy being sexually active.

Masturbation
during intercourse

At least 50 percent of women need stimulation over and above that of intercourse in order to reach orgasm. This means that relying on penetration alone is not enough. However, there are many additions to lovemaking that make sex more exciting. In fact, 82 percent of women

can climax from masturbation alone, which means you certainly shouldn't underestimate the sensitivity of your hands and fingers.

- Try stimulating her clitoris with your fingers during intercourse. Although your hand feels at an unnatural angle, it can often give just enough extra sensation to flip her right over into climax.
- If your wrist can't cope with the twist involved, try using a vibrator. You can wedge a vibrator so that it not only buzzes up against the clitoris but also vibrates against you and feels really good. Some male vibrators, in the shape of cock rings, are specially designed to give clitoral stimulation.
- Try the hand-riding technique. She puts a guiding hand on top of yours while you masturbate her. This way she can show you exactly how fast and how firmly she likes to be touched.
- If she's really sensitive, stroke her gently with your fingertip through fabric.

Slowing him down

We've covered how men can apply the "squeeze" technique in **Prolonging the pleasure** (page 194), but a woman can do the squeeze, too, with his cooperation. When he recognizes that he is nearing "the point of no return," he must tell you. You instantly withdraw from intercourse and, grasping his penis, squeeze it on the upper and lower side of the coronal ridge (around the head), thereby blocking off the ejaculation. Then stimulate him, either manually or with oral sex, until he regains his erection.

The rear approach

If he wants to control his climax himself, another method is to reach around behind yourself just before that "point of no return" and pull down hard on the testicles.

This also blocks the ejaculation. If he is not too certain about this, the pull can be practiced privately during self-stimulation.

Last resort

There are some guys who climax so rapidly that it happens at penetration itself or even before. All is not lost. Beta-blocker drugs, like propranolol, do a great job in slowing men down. Such drugs can be prescribed by a doctor.

Tantric sex

The aim of Tantric stroking is to give your partner a light touch all over the body, taking several days in which to cover the entire body. What makes Tantric stroking different from ordinary massage is that you are encouraged to tune into your partner's body as you feel it beneath your hands.

With each stroke, imagine that you are your partner receiving that stroke. After a while the experience of touch should become so merged and mingled in your head that you don't know which is you and which is your lover.

Eventually you graduate to Tantric containment, which is intercourse but without the thrusting. She simply lies motionless on top of him, penis in vagina, until the erection subsides.

Tantric intercourse aims to prolong sexual arousal. The penis penetrates the vagina by only an inch or so, stays there for a full minute, withdraws, and rests on the clitoral hood for a further minute, then slides back in.

For the next sequence of strokes, the penis rests on the outside of the vulva and subsequently just inside it.

What's the point?

If the stroking has been done thoroughly, you should have reached a state of total and exquisite arousal and, in theory, will be able to prolong this incredible sensation for hours.

Feeling fit for sex

Being in good shape is definitely of benefit when it comes to sex. There are three major factors that affect health, and have a direct impact on sexual performance.

Alcohol

Too much alcohol can lead to impotence, a lack of sensation, and sterility. "Brewer's droop" is a reality. Alcohol actually depresses the hormone testosterone. So stay off the booze, or at least drink only small amounts.

Tobacco

People who smoke smell disgusting to those who don't. Heavy smoking affects the arteries, which in turn can affect sexual performance. Heavy smoking is also thought to impair sperm production.

Exercise

Sexual intercourse demands a degree of physical fitness, so it helps to have healthy lungs, stamina, and not to be too overweight. Try to walk or swim regularly, eat high-fiber, low-fat foods, and consider taking up weight-lifting, martial arts, or Pilates to promote body strength.

Older loving

As we grow older, it is normal for men and women to experience less sexual sensation. On a practical level, this means that both partners may need more friction, time, patience, and different types of stimulation. Since you are also likely to have a little less energy, different types of sex positions can help.

The grind

In this position, once the man has moved up close against his partner's genitals he stays there, moving in small circles hard against her. This often helps stimulate her clitoris easily and means he doesn't have to work quite so hard at thrusting.

The clamp

The woman lies underneath with her legs tightly held together. As he penetrates her, he meets the extra pressure of her squeezing thighs, giving him a much longer run of firm sensation.

Sex from the rear

This can be helpful if she has a problem since he can easily stimulate her by hand from the front while penetrating from behind.

An extra boost

- Vibrators are very useful for providing the extra stimulation needed by more mature lovers.
- Menopausal women may find hormone replacement therapy (HRT) helpful, since the extra estrogen promotes youthful genital tissue and lubrication.
- Testosterone replacement therapy can help both men and women who have suffered a loss of sensual sensation (see also **Sex pills**, p.218).

Warmth moves

- Look into a partner's eyes for longer than normal.
- Move toward the other person so that you are closer than you would normally be.
- Smile more than usual, looking in turn at various parts of the body.
- Nod your head in vigorous agreement.
- When sitting down, make sure your body language is open (don't cross your arms or legs, for example).
- When talking, use hand gestures that take in your partner or indicate an appreciation of him/her.
- Take quick glances at the other person and, while doing so, moisten your lips with your tongue and widen your eyes a little.
- Make small touching movements. For example, when you stand together, move behind your partner, cuddling lightly against his/her body, with both arms around the waist. Or put an arm around your partner and caress and massage his/her back.

Impotence solutions

It is normal to experience occasional incidences of impotence. But sometimes the problem persists, which is when you might think of seeking help.

Little blue pill

One of the most popular aids is Viagra. This small blue pill stimulates erection – provided you think sexy thoughts to begin with. Sometimes, using Viagra just once or twice is enough to do the trick and get you functioning normally again. But Viagra is not for everyone. People with heart problems are warned not to take it. And if you have a difficulty known as venous leakage, it just doesn't work.

Penis ring

This medical sex aid can help if you experience venous leakage, which is when you can get an erection at first, but it seems to drain away. The reason that this happens is often because the "locking device" at the base of the penis fails, so the blood that rushes in to create an erection simply flows away again. The specially designed penis ring works by doing the "locking" for you.

Warning! Do not experiment with rubber bands; these could be dangerous.

Sex counseling

Sometimes impotence happens as a result of something going wrong in a relationship. In such situations, sex therapy can help couples talk about the issue and go on to practice a type of erotic homework aimed at getting sex going again.

Sex **pills**

If only there were a magic pill we could pop that would solve every sex problem. There isn't yet a particular "wonder" cure – but there are several new drugs that can help a variety of sexual difficulties. All such drugs must be medically prescribed.

Viagra

This little blue pill can help with impotence (see **Impotence solutions** page 216).

Beta-blockers

Drugs such as propranolol can deal with anxiety and can significantly delay ejaculation.

Phentolamine

Women who have problems "letting go" during sex might be interested to know that this drug works on the brain to lessen inhibition, thereby allowing desire to be fully expressed.

Testosterone

This hormone can be used by men and women and is rubbed into the skin in gel form to substantially increase libido, local sensation, and experience of orgasm.

Reading sexual **body language**

Learn how to deduce from your partner's body language what kind of a mood he or she is in.

Nervousness

- Your partner sits up in bed waiting for you. She is hunched forward, staring straight down at the bedclothes and clasping her hands tightly around her knees.
- This should tell you that she is feeling tense; she may be wondering if she is doing the right thing.

The best solution is to get into bed and give her a big, affectionate hug.

Anxiety

- Your partner hasn't followed through on the sexy preliminaries immediately but is rushing in and out of the bathroom, neatly hanging up clothes and brushing teeth. He/she takes an eternity.

The best solution is to avoid making any immediate sexual moves. Hold him/her in your arms. Wait until sensuality returns naturally.

Discomfort

♥ Your partner is lying next to you but is very stiff. This may indicate that he/she feels terribly responsible for what is about to happen.

The best solution is to offer a good massage. It indicates you know what to do, which in itself is reassuring, and massage feels physically good.

Inhibition

♥ On getting into bed, your partner turns his/her back on you and curls into a fetal position. This may indicate fear or strong emotion.

Try a spoonstyle hug and match your breathing to his/hers. This should help. But don't rush your partner into sex if he/she does not unwind.

Taking the **sexological** exam

This is an exercise designed to help you discover the geography of each other's genitals. It needs to be done in absolute privacy.

Him

- ♥ Stroke her breasts and nipples, noting any swelling or arousal. Ask if she has any preferences of touch.
- ♥ Examine her genitals. Touch her labia on the outside, then inside, then on the base, then on the top. As you do so, ask if this is an area that feels sensual or not.

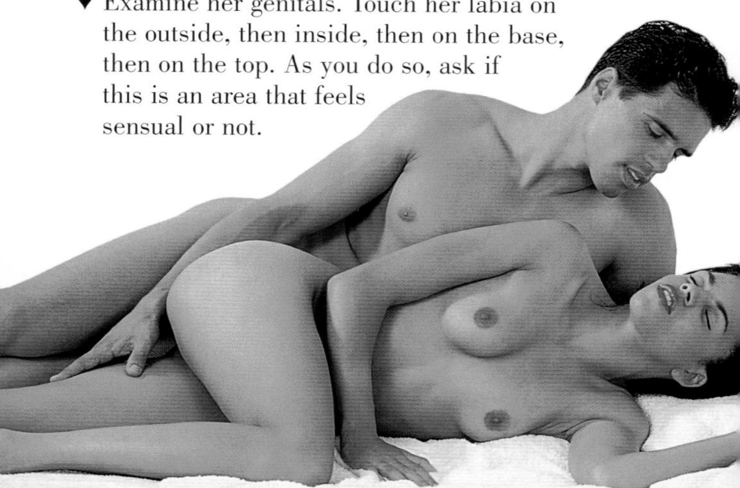

- ♥ Examine her anus. Imagine this to be a clock and press at various positions around it. The 10 o'clock point and the 2 o'clock point tend to be the most sensitive areas.
- ♥ Give your partner a mirror so that she can see what you have been discovering.

Her

- ♥ Stroke his nipples to ascertain response.
- ♥ Examine his pubic hair pattern. Extensive pubic hair growth is indicative of the greatest amount of free-ranging testosterone in the body.
- ♥ Hold the penis and examine its shape and appearance. If he is circumcized, see if he has experienced scarring and ask how this affects sensitivity.
- ♥ If he is uncircumcized, ask him to show you how he moves back his foreskin.
- ♥ Check your partner's urethra, the tiny slit in the head of the penis. If he is healthy it should be a good red colour.
- ♥ Examine his anus (in the same way he examined yours, see above).

The **sex history** exercise

The way in which we perceive parental relationships often gives important clues to how we see our own relationships and how we view sex. So it makes sense to share our life story with a partner, including the sexual details. If you contrast the ways in which you and your partner learned about sex, you will get a good idea of the joys and the challenges that lay ahead. Good luck!

Questions to ask

- ♥ What was your family's background? What were the occupation, religion, and culture of family members?
- ♥ What were their moral attitudes and their views on enjoyment and play?
- ♥ Were your parents and family affectionate toward each other, or tense and aggressive?
- ♥ What do you remember of incidents that may relate to your parents' sex life?
- ♥ What attitude did they have toward nudity?

- What kind of hidden messages do you think you received from your parents about sex?
- When and how did you first learn about sex?
- When did you first masturbate?
- Do you have sexual fantasies? If you do, at what age did they begin?
- Did you or do you have crushes on people of the same sex?
- If you are a man, how old were you when you first had wet dreams?
- If you are a woman, at what age did you start menstruation?
- What was your earliest sexual experience? Same sex or opposite sex?
- What have your subsequent sexual experiences and relationships been like?

Romantic reminiscences

It doesn't matter how crazily in love you are at the start of a relationship. This kind of love is only a temporary state, and after about six months to two years, the first euphoria will have worn off – if you're fortunate, you'll be left with bonds of deep affection.

This change inevitably affects the experience of sex, although it will probably still work well – even if you do not find time for it so often. Sometimes, the fading of an intense passion can become a problem.

One exercise that helps rekindle that initial flame is reminiscing. Remembering those romantic first moments can bring back some of the sparkle. Everyone likes hearing those feelings spoken out loud again after a gap of years. And such memories rekindle warm feelings.

Questions to ask yourself and your partner

- ♥ What is your first romantic memory of this person?
- ♥ What did you first fancy about your partner in a sexual sense?
- ♥ What were the first moves he/she made toward you?
- ♥ What is your best memory of early romance?
- ♥ What happened the first time he/she touched you?
- ♥ What is your first memory of sex with your partner?

The **stepping** exercise

The idea of stepping is to try to resolve a problem in small steps. Where sex is concerned, you might go for a whole body massage first, then a massage that includes the genitals, then a massage that focuses less on the whole body and more on the genitals, then concentrating on the genitals for longer to see if this leads to orgasm.

Go back a step

Some people find they get to a particular point and then panic. Best method here is to go back a step, enjoy what you managed before but talk about your fears. Why might this be a sticking point? Is there anything your partner might do to reassure you? Are there alternative techniques that might be more acceptable?

Work from a list

Write a list of actions you want to take, number them in order of difficulty, then work your way up, from the easiest to the most difficult. If something proves too tough, just go back a step, regain your confidence, then try again. It can be surprisingly effective!

The power of **emotions**

Anger

- ♥ Can improve sexual response since the arousal in one brain site sometimes leaks over into the next, which happens to be a sex site. Hey, presto! Turn-on.
- ♥ However, some people cannot feel both angry and sexy at the same time. Perhaps a degree of anger is stimulating, but if anger increases, leading to resentment and more powerful feelings of rage, then desire will be eroded.
- ♥ Avoidance or rejection of sexual activity may be a way of expressing anger.

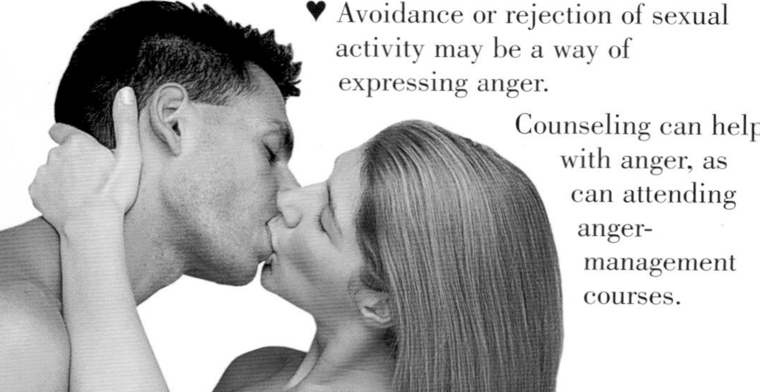

Counseling can help with anger, as can attending anger-management courses.

Anxiety

- ♥ Can interfere with sexual response – it either speeds it up or slows it down.
- ♥ Can interfere with the thought processes that help you make a reasoned assessment of a situation, so may therefore impede your ability to improve it.
- ♥ Can be a reaction to some sexual failure.
- ♥ Can make response easier!

Cognitive behavioral therapy can help with anxiety, as can beta-blocker drugs.

Depression

- ♥ Lowers sexual desire.
- ♥ Impairs erection in men.
- ♥ Impairs erection and lubrication in women.
- ♥ Makes orgasm difficult to reach.

Depression can be alleviated through therapy, where you talk about your problems in conjunction with antidepressants.

Ten **thoughts** to remember

1 Nice guys finish last.

2 Nice women initiate sex often.

3 Sensitive partners pick up on a new partner's anxiety or inhibition, offer warm hugs as reassurance, and take things very slowly.

4 If either partner is unsure as to how the other's sexuality works, he or she asks.

5 It is good to give feedback, provided that it is done sensitively.

6 Lovemaking is not always appropriate. Both partners should be picking up on the other's mood before suggesting sex.

7 Good partners make each other feel wonderful about themselves.

8 It is never appropriate to use someone for sex, then leave.

9 No one should ever be pressured into doing something he/she blatantly doesn't want to do.

10 If someone is drunk, he/she should not, under any circumstances, be taken advantage of sexually.

The **yes/no** exercise

The yes/no exercise involves saying "yes" to three things you really want to do and "no" to three things you really don't want to do within a one-week timeframe.

The purpose of the exercise is to make you more aware of your priorities in life and to build up enough courage to actively work at achieving what you want.

You can interpret the exercise in a small way by saying "yes" to a chocolate bar even though you shouldn't really eat it because you really want it. Or you could say "no" to a chocolate bar because slimming is a true priority.

Alternatively, you could really take the exercise seriously, as Claire did:

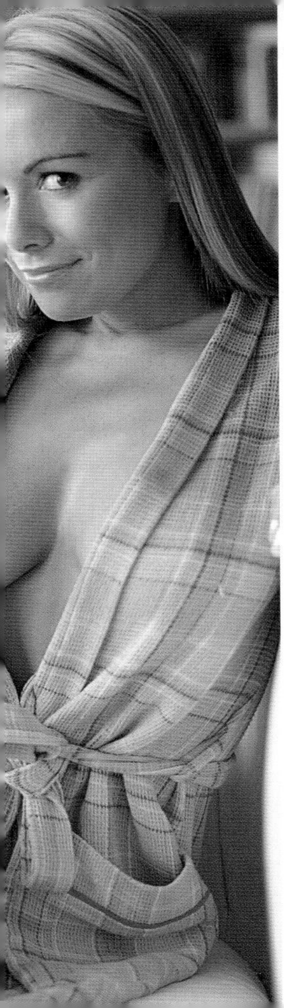

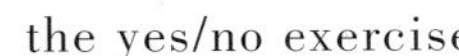

- Claire said "no" to her old job and "yes" to getting a new one.
- She said "no" to sharing an apartment with roommates she disliked and "yes" to going out and getting an apartment all to herself.
- Finally, she said "no" to her current boyfriend because she realized that she really didn't like him and was going out with him only because there was no one else and "yes" to preferring life on her own.

In the space of a week, Claire actually changed her life. It was no accident that she subsequently learned how to climax and ended up with a former male friend whom she eventually married.

Index

N O

P

R S

T V

W Y

Acknowledgments

Photography: Luc Beziat, Mark Harwood, Alastair Hughes, Peter Pugh-Cook, James Muldowney, Jules Selmes

All images © Dorling Kindersley. For further information see www.dkimages.com

Props: *Ann Summers* for the loan of lingerie and sex aids. *Skin Two* for the loan of pvc outfits

For good-quality sex aids try:

UK

Harmony
167 Charing Cross Rd London
WC2H 0EN
and:
4 Walkers Court
London W1R 3FQ

Passion8
NES.,
PO Box 88
Hull HU5 5FW
Tel: 01482 873377

Ann Summers
For you nearest store, or to organize a party, telephone 020 8645 8320 or visit the website: www.annsummers.com

Skin Two (for pvc and bondage equipment)
Tel: 020 7735 7195

US

Good Vibrations
1210 Valencia St
San Francisco
CA 94110
Tel: (415) 974 8980
www.goodvibes.com

Australia

The Tool Shed
Call (02) 9360 1100 or Toll Free on 1800 181 069 (outside Sydney) for your nearest shop in Sydney, or visit the website to view their selection of toys, accessories and clothing: www.thetoolshed.com.au